HITLER IN LIVERPOOL
and Other Plays

ii

By the same Author

You'll Come to Love Your Sperm Test (in *New Writers 4*)
Trixie and Baba
Why Bournemouth? (also *An Apple a Day* and *The Missing Links*)

PLAYSCRIPT 100

HITLER IN LIVERPOOL
One Orange for the Baby
Up in the Hide

John Antrobus

RIVERRUN

John
Calder

JOHN CALDER · LONDON
RIVERRUN PRESS · NEW YORK

iv

Hitler in Liverpool and Other Plays first published in Great Britain, 1983, by
John Calder (Publishers) Ltd.,
18 Brewer Street,
London W1R 4AS

and in USA, 1983, by
Riverrun Press,
175 Fifth Avenue,
New York NY10010

British Library Cataloguing in Publication Data

Antrobus, John
   Hitler in Liverpool and other plays:-
   (Playscript series; 100)
   822'.914

SUBSIDISED BY THE
Arts Council
OF GREAT BRITAIN

ISBN 0 7145 3898 1 paperbound

Typeset in 9/10pt on Scantaxt 1000 by Gedset, Cheltenham
Printed and bound by Hillman Printers (Frome) Ltd., Somerset

CONTENTS

INTRODUCTION

John Antrobus trundled up the stairs of the Gate, Notting Hill and cornered me. 'I saw the face of a friend of mine on a poster on the front door of your theatre [Dudley Sutton, who was appearing in *The Empire Builders* at the time] so I thought it was safe to come in. I'd like to suggest that your entire Spring season be devoted to all of my unperformed plays.' I was about to usher him down the stairs when he handed me a huge pile of scripts and said 'I'm John Antrobus and this place really excites me.'

What happened next was a season called The John Antrobus Season and a collaboration in which John worked with me as actor (*Hitler in Liverpool*), director (*One Orange for the Baby*), and playwright in residence in one of the most prolific, engaging, and manic ten weeks I have ever spent. All in all, these three world premieres, with its talented company of fifteen actors working in a small studio space, made its own kind of history.

The first play of the season, *Hitler in Liverpool*, was the flagship play of the season. Although we didn't get the expected hordes of protestors in Notting Hill against a play about the young Hitler, John, who played Hitler's brother Alois, provided enough excitement and controversy. The play takes place in Liverpool in 1912 where Alois runs a small restaurant and is married to Liverpudlian actress, Bridget Hitler. It begins with a visit from Alois' down-and-out younger brother, Adolf, aged 24. Watching John romp through the scenes was pure joy — even if John was prone to unveiling new surprises each night. On one occasion, the dramatic muse had so possessed him that in the scene where he lends his threadbare brother Adolf his jacket, John stripped right down to his long woolly underpants accompanied with a bravura improvisation declaring brotherly devotion.

While *Hitler in Liverpool* ran in the evenings, John rehearsed the company in the mornings for *One Orange for the Baby* while I rehearsed the same company in the afternoon for *Up in the Hide*.

This arrangement proved to be a grave error. For the first week of rehearsals, I would arrive fresh and full of energy only to find a company of exhausted actors — some of whom nodded off during a few of my more inventive rehearsals. Something was wrong.

I dropped in on one of John's morning rehearsals only to find that he had the company shindigging and twisting madly for hours on end to the music of the Beach Boys and the Beatles, blasting away on the house sound system. 'They have to develop stamina for the actual performance of the final party scene,' he explained. He then retreated to the director's place at the rear of the theatre and continued watching them dance while writing more party dialogue for them. The scene, needless to say, was brilliantly written and staged by John — and they did develop the necessary stamina to dance and talk non-stop for a half hour in a kind of pressurized Robert Altman miniature on stage. And in the end, the contrast of my rehearsal techniques for *Up in the Hide* made the whole experience an exciting one.

When the season finished, its sheer intensity created a glow in the theatre which lasted for some time. Over the past few years John has remained closely associated with the Gate. We subsequently produced his comedy thriller *Looneys*, and, more recently, *The Bedsitting Room II*, re-vamped and directed by John himself at the new Gate at the Latchmere in Battersea. This was the first revival of the play since its premiere at the Mermaid in the sixties.

These plays are exemplary of the best of John's work: extraordinary and unusual in his balance of absurd comedy and his observations of English life. His style is always fresh and surprising.

Lou Stein

HITLER IN LIVERPOOL

x

Characters

ALOIS HITLER
BRIDGET HITLER
ADOLF HITLER
ANNIE
DOCTOR SPHLITZ
BARON VON MINSKIN
VALET
RAZOR MAN
TRAMP
PORTER
POLICEMAN
POLICE INSPECTOR
Passengers, Strangers, Street musicians

First night at the Gate Theatre, London, 10th March 1980. Directed by Lou Stein. Designed by Jim Daly.

ADOLF HITLER	Richard Bremmer
ALOIS HITLER	John Antrobus
BRIDGET HITLER	Margaret Ashley
ANNIE WATKINS	Sharon McKevitt
DR SPHLITZ	Tony Guilfoyle
BARON VON MINSKIN	Mike Burnside
RAZOR MAN	Anthony Sergeant
POLICE INSPECTOR	Anthony Sergeant
TRAMP	Martin Kennedy
PORTER	Martin Kennedy
VALET	Kevin Pearcy
PASSENGERS ON TRAIN AND PASSERS-BY	Mike Burnside Tony Guilfoyle Martin Kennedy

ACT ONE

Scene 1

Lime Street station. November 1912. Enter ALOIS *and* BRIDGET.

ALOIS *(looks at his watch)*. Ach! The train is late ... unless my watch is wrong.... My watch is wrong ... it's three hours fast.... I bought if off an Arab ... he's sending me on the works later.... What a beautiful evening it is....

BRIDGET. It's a horrible evening...

ALOIS. That is so ... which is why it's so amazing it is so beautiful.... Ah so.... Look at that roof — look at the intricate structure of iron work ... is it any wonder I'm so enthusiastic....

BRIDGET. I hope Angela got the ticket alright....

ALOIS. She would have received the money for the ticket....

BRIDGET. You trust your relatives, don't you?

ALOIS. Yah ... We are doing a great thing giving Angela a holiday ... I use the term 'we' because ... through strictly speaking we are separate people — united in giving Angela a holiday — We have a common intent expressed by the sending of the money, yah? Though we are diverse human beings of a different sex ... with entirely different backgrounds yah ... Yet in the coming together of the sending of this money the two have become one ... I don't think so ... I cherish the fact that I am a separate human being ... and were it not for you I would still want Angela to come here ...

BRIDGET. It's alright by me luv....

ALOIS. Yah — even if it were not alright by you she would be coming here I'm telling you....

BRIDGET. It's alright by me.

ALOIS. Yah — that I know — what I'm saying is — in the face of the stiffest opposition from you my sister would be coming to us.

BRIDGET. I never said a word.

ALOIS. That is so.... You are against the safety razor?

BRIDGET. Oh don't bring that up again....

ALOIS. You do not believe it is safe? Have I not demonstrated it to you Bridget? Will you not trust the safety razor, Bridget, as a sign of faith in your husband?

BRIDGET. I won't use it on my legs.

ALOIS. There is a fortune in the safety razor. What a nice evening it is.

BRIDGET. A fortune to be lost, Alois.

ALOIS. That is what they say about all great inventions ... the flying machine ... the tram.

BRIDGET. It's a mistake not to have the horses . . . you can't hear 'em coming.

ALOIS. You can hear the tram.

BRIDGET. You can't hear the hooves.

ALOIS. The safety razor is a boon to mankind . . . it will save time . . . time in the morning for a man is most important . . . He will not have to be stropping for three minutes each side . . . That is six minutes times three hundred and sixty-five for one year.

BRIDGET. Don't put any of our money into it. . . . You agreed you wouldn't.

ALOIS. You'll be sorry. . . .

A MAN *enters. There are bits of plaster all over his face. He wears a long mac, and looks a bit dissolute. He beckons furtively to* ALOIS.

ALOIS *(to* BRIDGET*).* Excuse me. . . . *(Goes to* MAN*)* Why are you following me everywhere? *(The* MAN *takes safety razor from mac pocket.)*

MAN. It don't work wack.

ALOIS. What do you mean it don't work? Were you using soap?

MAN. You 'ave to use soap?

ALOIS. Give it one more week trial — report back. . . .

MAN. Where's me pound?

ALOIS. Not yet.

MAN. I'm bleeding to death here. (*ALOIS snatches razor from him.*)

ALOIS. Use soap . . . and you must turn this little knob at the bottom.

MAN. What? While I'm shaving?

ALOIS. No — before. So that the blade is tight in the fit . . .

MAN. Can't you manage ten bob? I'm dying for a drink. (ALOIS *gives him ten bob, and the razor back.*)

ALOIS. It will work.

MAN. I hope so . . . I'm terrified. . . . *(He leaves.)*

BRIDGET. Who was that?

ALOIS. A working man on hard times. . . .

BRIDGET. What's wrong with his face?

ALOIS. A terrible disease . . . poverty.

BRIDGET. Annie's looking after the baby like . . . she's gonna be awful late home.

ALOIS. There is a Mr Smith — who has invented a crisp . . . Bridget. . . .

BRIDGET. I don't want to catch you tickling that Annie's tits . . . not no more I don't. *(*TRAMP *enters — playing flute. Talking over flute)* If I catch you tickling her tits you'll answer to me.

ALOIS. Vot? If I am tickling her tits *you* will answer? You are on the other end of her tits eh! *(Laughs.)* I was testing out her garments . . . there is a fortune in the brazziere . . . it is under-developed . . . suiting some figures I may add. Vot is the matter with you Bridget?

BRIDGET. Tell that man to go away. *(*ALOIS *puts coin in* TRAMPS'S *hat.* TRAMP *picks up hat and exits.)* Did you pay him? I didn't say pay him anything.

ALOIS. Who is giving the orders round here? I have been down on my uppers . . . maybe I will need a coin again sometime.

BRIDGET. I'm sure you will.

ALOIS.   What we need is a war . . . a war with Japan — it would be good for
trade . . . the whole world needs war. Ve have not had a good war for a long
while.

BRIDGET.   What about the Boer war then?

ALOIS.   What about the Boer war. . . . You call that a war? I am talking about a
big war. Where men can prove themselves . . . not to be domestic animals.

BRIDGET.   You frighten me with that talk.

ALOIS.   Blood must be shed . . . or we all go to the worldhouse on a penny a
day. . . . Where do men find comradeship? In battle. Where do men find
hatred? In battle. where do men find love? Not here. I would not be a coward
in war. I would find cowardice . . . but I would not be bana. . . .

BRIDGET.   Have you been writing to your brother again?

ALOIS.   Vot?

BRIDGET.   Have you been writing to Adolf? It sounds like you've got hold of
his half-baked ideas.

ALOIS.   My brother and I do not talk to each other now. . . . When I am coming out of prison and I write home to Vienna for money — he writes back 'go
hang yourself' . . . that is my brother — that is not from my mother — she
signed the letter but he wrote it . . . he dictated it. . .

BRIDGET.   You have to stand on your own two feet Alois.

ALOIS.   Why should I? Vy can't I stand on your feet? On anybody's feet?
Maybe I haven't got feet of my own.

BRIDGET.   You've got money now . . . hang onto it . . . no more hairbrained
schemes . . . you got me and the baby now.

ALOIS.   I have will power . . . I have the life force in me Bridget. You will die
before I stop living.

The sound of a train drawing in.

BRIDGET.   Is that the train? Is that it? *(louder)* From London! Is that it? *(A
PORTER crosses stage with trolley.)*

ALOIS.   Is that the London train please?

PORTER.   Aye, that's your lot tonight! That's the last one in! An' we close the
waiting-room after this wack! Ain't you got a home to go to?

ALOIS.   I am well dressed.

PORTER.   That's what they all say! Want a warm by the pipes — you better get
in there while there's a chance! *(ALOIS grabs his collar.)*

ALOIS.   I am well dressed! How dare you insult my suit!

PORTER.   I'm sorry . . . I'm — sorry.

ALOIS.   Kiss my suit! Kiss it! Feel the cloth! Now am I spending the night in
your stinking waiting-room!

PORTER.   I didn't know you was a foreigner. . . . Friend of Bismark are yer?
Beg pardon your highness! *(ALOIS lets PORTER go.)*

ALOIS.   My suit cost five pound.

PORTER *exits. Hissing of steam, as train clanks to halt.* BRIDGET *has stepped
away to look for passengers coming off train.*

BRIDGET *(has not seen porter fracas).*   What's she look like again? *(she is
peering over the barrier.)*

ALOIS.   Red faced.

Passengers are coming off the train and passing by — offstage.

BRIDGET.   There's a lot of luggage! What does her luggage look like?
ALOIS.   Smart! Very smart. . . .
BRIDGET *(calls out — off — leaning over barrier).*   Stop that luggage *(arguing with someone)* I don't care whose it is! Well stay by it if its yours! Stop showing off! Fathead!

Two upper-class PASSENGERS *come through, with* PORTER *pushing luggage.*

FIRST PASSENGER.   There'll be war by Christmas. . . . The Sudan is in a turmoil.
SECOND PASSENGER.   Ever was so.
FIRST PASSENGER.   The natives are trying to buy guns from the Italians.
SECOND PASSENGER.   Then we must sell them to the Italians — if we don't someone else will.
FIRST PASSENGER.   That's where the profit lies.
SECOND PASSENGER.   Ever was so. . . .
PORTER *(shouts off).*   Cab! Cabby!
FIRST PASSENGER.   I'd be willing to die in the Sudan to put those blighters down.
SECOND PASSENGER.   Well let's arm them first . . . make a scrap of it. . . . *(They leave)*
BRIDGET.   I can't see her . . . not like you describe her. . . .

ADOLF HITLER *enters — exhausted. Poverty stricken. No luggage. He walks past* BRIDGET. ALOIS *has been listening to the* PASSENGERS. *Turns and sees his brother.*

ALOIS.   Adolf! (ADOLF *takes hold of* ALOIS' *sleeve. Talks into his ear.*) I see. . . . Yes. . . . Alright . . . welcome. . . . *(*BRIDGET *notices them.)* Bridget . . . this is Adolf Hitler . . . my brother. . . .
BRIDGET.   Where's Angela?
ALOIS.   She couldn't come. . . . He didn't want to disappoint us. . . . *(*HITLER *slowly turns and looks at* BRIDGET.)*
ADOLF.   Bridget Hitler?
BRIDGET.   Yes. . . . *(They stare at each other.)*
ALOIS.   Welcome to Liverpool, Adolf. . . . Where is your luggage? *(*HITLER *stands there looking absolutely shattered — aside to* BRIDGET*)* He has no luggage . . . poor man. . . . *(He embraces* HITLER.*)* Let's go home. . . .

He leads HITLER *off.* BRIDGET *follows.*

Scene 2

The next morning. The modest apartment of ALOIS *and* BRIDGET. ADOLF HITLER *is asleep on the couch. Enter* ALOIS. *He tucks* ADOLF'S *blankets in. Enter* BRIDGET *— feeling baby-bottle against her cheek.*

ALOIS.   I am so glad to see him, you know that . . . My heart has gone out to him . . . the poor wretch — my brother — may God forgive me for the hardness of heart that I have shown him.

BRIDGET.   It wasn't all one way. . . . He told you to go hang yourself.

ALOIS.   That was a tiff . . . a family tiff.

BRIDGET.   He can't sleep there forever.

ALOIS.   He's exhausted.

BRIDGET.   I mean this is our living room Alois. . . . How long's he intend to stay?

ALOIS.   I. . . . I have not yet discussed his plans . . . first he must recuperate Bridget. . . .

BRIDGET.   We haven't got much room here.

ALOIS.   I know we have not got much room. They did not have much room at the inn. You are a Catholic.

BRIDGET.   I'm not being hard . . .

ALOIS.   After a few days we will discover his plans — and help him on his way. I realize that we have not much room . . . but to see him this way. . . . *(BRIDGET picks up his shirt.)*

BRIDGET.   I can't turn this collar.

ALOIS.   Give him one of my shirts please. . . . Well I must be going out for a little while. . . .

BRIDGET.   Don't leave me here. I don't know him, Alois. I don't speak his language.

ALOIS.   Compassion. . . .

BRIDGET.   How can we help him?

ALOIS.   We'll find out. . . .

BRIDGET.   He mustn't become a burden to us . . . we've got the baby now.

ALOIS.   The milk of human kindness.

BRIDGET.   I hope he don't frighten the baby.

ALOIS.   What?

BRIDGET.   Looking like that.

ALOIS.   He will soon have a shave . . . I'll lend him a *safety* razor . . . Bridget . . . Adolf may be the best man to be my agent in Europe . . . my sales director. This may be a blessing in disguise. Adolf Hitler could be the man with the safety razor in Germany . . . it could spread like wildfire . . . if he has the personality . . . I don't know that. . . .

BRIDGET.   You haven't sold the restaurant, have you? There's been so much coming and going.

ALOIS.   There are a million restaurants . . . there is one safety razor.

BRIDGET.   It's a gold mine . . . it's our little restaurant . . . you put all your savings into it.

ALOIS.   There is not room for expansion . . . a man must expand or die. I must have Lebensraum. I must attempt . . . not to attempt Bridget is to fail. . . .

BRIDGET.   I hope your brother can talk some sense into you.

ALOIS.   Yes he's the quiet one of the family . . . I'm the black sheep . . . he's the goody. Nursed mother on her deathbed. God bless him for that . . . never left her side. I couldn't do it. Yes he's the good one . . . he's a saint alright. I am the bad one in the family. I am the bad penny . . . in and out of jail. . . .

BRIDGET.   All that's behind you.

ALOIS.   He was right to tell me go hang myself. I nearly did . . . but I forgive
   him for it. Yes he is good. I am bad . . . but I am not evil. I mean I am kind
   where I am able to be kind. . . . But I cannot stick at anything you know that.
   Adolf — he has perseverance — he is an artist — we have an artist in the family . . . good . . . that is why he is this way — he is suffering for his art. Perhaps
   it is good for him. . . . He makes postcards — for a living — it is modest — it is
   not the Sistine Chapel my God — but give him time. . . . Give him time my
   brother! You see a man who is dying for his art. Do you know he is a frustrated
   architect? He is educating himself. He is making himself into a person . . . this
   much I know. The world is against him . . . the world is against such as he and
   myself. I am no good — I will steal — if that is the easiest way — I steal from the
   poor — they're used to being stolen against — they won't notice. . . . Bridget,
   that is not strictly true — I am not without compassion. I broke into one house
   in Berlin — it was a mistake . . . they were so poor. I went back the next night
   with a food hamper . . . that's how it is. You can't always tell from the outside.
   I have seen things, Bridget, that would make your hair stand on end . . . I have
   mixed with the poor and the desolate — I have been one with them. I am with
   them now — Give him two shirts — give him all my shirts. . . . My suit? Give
   him my suit! That I should be so attached to a garment — it is to my shame —
   what is happening to me. If I do not taste poverty I am not a man. Give me
   war. . . . Give me my brother. He is a half-brother? There is no such thing. . . .
   I will invent — I will get rich quick. I will get poor quick? Maybe . . . I don't
   care.
BRIDGET.   We must build for the future.
ALOIS.   Build? Build what? A coffin? Feed him well Bridget — while he is
   with us. Fatten him up . . . I will look after the family.
BRIDGET.   What about our family? What will we eat tomorrow?
ALOIS.   What will they eat today?
BRIDGET.   We must look after ourselves first . . . you frighten me.
ALOIS.   There is nothing to look after. There is no tomorrow to look after. It is
   never there.
BRIDGET.   You and your fancy ideas. If you sell that restaurant we're
   through. Take your blasted brother and get out of here both of you.
ALOIS.   Bridget.
BRIDGET.   I'm sorry . . . but your ideas spell ruin. . . . And now there's two of
   you. . . .

She leaves. A knock on the door. ALOIS *opens it. Enter razor* MAN. *He holds a
blood stained handkerchief to his neck.*

MAN.   I'm bleeding . . . I'm bleeding like a pig. . . . Take your bloody razor —
   it'll never work. . . . Ere you are wack take it — you owe me ten bob more.
   Bloody foreigners. (*Dabbing with hanky*) Blood blood blood. . . .
ALOIS (*indicates he should be quiet*).   Did you use soap?
MAN.   I used lots of soap.
ALOIS.   Did you work up a good lather. . . .
MAN.   One of the best . . . you can't fault me there wack. I'm cutting me own
   throat for one of your mad experiments. 'Cos I need the money — is that
   right?
ALOIS.   We can't talk here.

MAN.   I won't be able to talk anywhere. *(Takes out razor.)* Take this devilish
    machine . . . where'd you get it?
ALOIS.   I have the licence . . .
MAN.   Licence . . . licence to kill. I should be replacing bodily fluids.
ALOIS.   Yah we will go down to the local. . . . Come mit me. Have faith . . .
    where is your faith? Blood? It must be shed — of course it must. . . . If you will
    die for the safety razor there will be others that will come after you. . . . Come
    — come we will replace the bodily fluids. . . . *(They exit. Pause.* HITLER *in
    his sleep — sits up — stares at we know not what.)*
ADOLF.   No! *(Pause.)* Nein . . . Nein . . . Nein. . . .

He covers his head with the blanket as he lies back again.

Scene 3

Later — in the apartment. ADOLF *is sitting up on the settee, wearing one of*
ALOIS' *shirts. He is dressed.* ALOIS *enters from kitchen with two mugs of tea.
Gives one to* ADOLF. *Gives him sugar bowl.* ADOLF *takes six spoonfuls of
sugar.*

BRIDGET *(voice off).*   Give us a hand up with the pram will yer!

ALOIS *exits.* ADOLF *sits there staring into space. Holding his tea, apparently
he has forgotten about it. Enter* ALOIS, *backing in with pram.* BRIDGET
enters after him.

ALOIS.   Bridget! Ahh . . . here we are all gathered! Has Adolf seen the baby
    yet?
BRIDGET.   No — he hasn't. . . . *(*BRIDGET *exits, wheeling pram to kit-
    chen.)*
ALOIS.   You have been shopping? That is good! *(Calling to* BRIDGET *in kit-
    chen)* I came home from work early today . . . business . . . business waits for
    no man — eh Adolf? And if it were not for the small businessman where
    would the big business be? For every big business was once the inspiration of
    the small man — except for the standing army. I am talking to Adolf for half
    an hour . . . *(looks at his watch)* precisely. . . . He is very interested in us —
    what we are doing — I have been telling him . . . about the safety razor and its
    remarkable future. I am asking him if there is any such thing in Germany — he
    ɔes not know. He is telling me Bridget that in the homeland now things are
    ery bad. . . . *(*BRIDGET *drifts in. Tidies up. A bit impatiently. Obviously
    ɪot used to having a guest in the sitting-room, that one has to live round.)* It
    ɪas been very bad for Adolf — the Jewish art dealers have been buying his
    work that is for sure — his postcards. At one stage he is living with a Jewish
    agent — and he has been drawing posters for him. He is very grateful, Adolf
    — it did not last. . . . He has been staying in a working men's club — Adolf.
    Where he has his own cubicle — with bed . . . mit chair and dressing table yah
    — and the po under the bed — all a man can want — that's all I want! Vy
    should I be domesticated? I tell you, Adolf lives the life of a saint — a very
    simple life.
BRIDGET.   What's he come over here for then?

ALOIS.   To visit us.

BRIDGET.   Oh ay.

ALOIS.   He did very much want to see the baby . . . and to meet you. As you know Angela could not come . . . and so he seized the opportunity, knowing he would be welcome. *(Looks at* BRIDGET *meaningfully.)* He has come to his brother's house. Things are very bad in Vienna right now.

BRIDGET.   They're very bad in Liverpool.

ALOIS.   It's no worse in Liverpool than it always was. . . . Yah that's bad. Adolf you are not drinking your tea. *(To* BRIDGET*)* I have told him I will speak English in front of you — that way will make him learn. *(To* ADOLF*)* Adolf *(Points at tea.)* A cup of tea *(Mimes drink.)* Drink. . . . *(*ADOLF *drinks his tea.)* Yah — dat is good. . . .

BRIDGET.   What's he going to do over here? Is he looking for a job then?

ALOIS.   Adolf is very interested in politics.

BRIDGET.   Does he want to get on the council then? We could do with a bit of life.

ALOIS.   Ya well maybe he could be on the Liverpool council yah — one day. He is very interested in the architecture.

BRIDGET.   Half these buildings need blowing up.

ALOIS.   Ya well maybe he could do that. . . He is very tired Bridget. Dis is not the time to talk of his career. . . .

BRIDGET.   Is he staying over here then? Is he looking for somewhere to stay? 'Cos Mrs Haddock down the road. . . .

ALOIS.   He is not looking for somewhere to stay. . . . He is staying with us.

BRIDGET.   That's what I mean — it's a visit?

ALOIS.   Yah it is a visit.

BRIDGET.   Then he won't want to be on the Liverpool council will he? If he's not staying long?

ALOIS.   No.

BRIDGET.   Only he don't look as though he's going anywhere. . ..

ALOIS.   He cannot understand what you are saying. . . .

BRIDGET.   He's welcome for a little while luv. We'll do what we can for him — he don't look well at all. Adolf you don't look at all well. *(To* ALOIS*)* Only when he's better if he's staying in the 'Pool he'll need to find lodgings.

ALOIS.   Yah.

BRIDGET.   Unless. . . .

ALOIS.   Yah yah. . . .

BRIDGET.   Unless he going back to — where you both come from. . . .

ALOIS.   Not a bad idea.

BRIDGET.   Only it'll mean him staying on the couch — we haven't got any where else. . . . I suppose that's alright . . . for a little while . . . I suppose . . . like he'll want to go back to Hunland for Christmas.

ALOIS.   Yah. . . .

BRIDGET.   In good time to do his shopping.

ALOIS.   Yah.

BRIDGET.   Only it's a bit inconvenient for your brother — us using this as a living room. . . .

ALOIS.   He won't mind that. . . . *(*ADOLF *dozes off.* ALOIS *rescues the tea.)*

BRIDGET.   He's like a dormouse isn't he? Pathetic. . . How did he get in that state?

ALOIS.   He is a dedicated man . . . as a boy . . . he . . . he read a lot — an awful lot.

BRIDGET.   Oh aye — well if that's what reading books does for you I'll stick to the papers.

ALOIS.   Bridget you are educated. You are an actress. I will put you back on the stage one day — it is in my plan.

BRIDGET.   You haven't got any more like him at home have you?

ALOIS.   No. Nein. He is travelling under his brother's name . . . Edmund. Edmund is dead.

BRIDGET.   Oh I see . . . that's how he was able to pass himself off.

ALOIS.   Edmund died many years ago. Adolf has taken his name for the passport.

BRIDGET.   Why?

ALOIS.   I don't know. Why? I don't know. Why?

BRIDGET.   For sentimental reasons?

ALOIS.   Hardly . . . Bridget.

BRIDGET.   I'll be nice to him, don't worry. But I don't want him staying too long. . . .

ALOIS.   He may soon be working as an artist. We do not know his long term plans do we?

BRIDGET.   No — we don't know what he's going to make of his life, that's for sure. But we can't have him hanging around here for long. . . . *(Pause — as she works.)* You paid for Angela to come over — your sister.

ALOIS.   She could not come.

BRIDGET.   Then why didn't they send the money back?

ALOIS.   For all I know Adolf is fleeing from the authorities. This vos his golden opportunity. Dey have the call-up in Austria — I don't think he was well enough to go to the medical.

BRIDGET.   If he went to the medical he'd be sure to fail.

ALOIS.   I don't think he was well enough to fail.

BRIDGET.   My God — what a world.

ALOIS.   In the army he would put on weight quickly . . . the trouble is getting into the army. He is not a coward . . . he vos not well enough to go to the medical. He vos sleeping rough — he was too ashamed to present himself . . . for service to the Fatherland.

BRIDGET.   He looks about just right for the British army . . . they'll take anyone. They took Alf Gas — they sent him to Ireland — he looks good now — he was a terrible mess.

ALOIS.   You think that Adolf should go to Ireland?

BRIDGET.   He could try the Black and Tans.

ALOIS.   Yah — but first he must learn the language.

BRIDGET.   I don't see why — no one'll talk to him. . . . Is he going to lie there all day? He's been glued to that settee — I haven't seen him off it since he come in, 'cept when he went to the bathroom — then he was too weak to open the door. I feel sorry for him — I do — I'll do what I can. But I don't want him staying long. If we're going to have to pay his fare back we'd better cut our losses and do it quick.

ALOIS.   He may not go back to Germany. Adolf Hitler, who knows . . . there may be no future for him in Germany. . . .

Scene 4

A week later. ADOLF *is trying on an overcoat, helped by* ALOIS. BRIDGET *stands in background.*

ALOIS. There you are Adolf — my coat fits you like a glove.

BRIDGET. I don't think he understands the intended pun.

ALOIS. Now today we are going for a walk yah.

BRIDGET. Why don't you tell him in German?

ALOIS. Nein — we would be talking German to each other all the while . . . I have made a rule . . . in your presence we only speak English . . . would I shut you off from the relationship with my brother. . . . *(*ADOLF *sits down on the settee, wearing coat.)* Don't sit down Adolf — we are going out. . . . *(*ADOLF *stays seated.)* We are going to the docks to see the British Merchant Fleet — he has expressed great interest in this . . . the might of the British navy yah?

BRIDGET. When's he emigrating to America then?

ALOIS. That was a suggestion — it came up in an ideas session.

BRIDGET. They take any riffraff — as long as they're healthy. *(Looks at* ADOLF.*)* He wouldn't get in would he? *(Aside to* ALOIS.*)* For God's sake get him out of here. He lives on that settee — he's rooted to it. I got the feeling we built the flat round him. I can't take it Alois — it's his presence. Either he goes or I go.

ALOIS. You need a break yah.

BRIDGET. I been walking the streets — with the baby an'all — for hours on end. I can't stand it with him in here. I can't invite anyone in, can I?

ALOIS. Why not?

BRIDGET. Ohh . . . *(acts out)* This is my brother-in-law — him and the settee go together. He won't look at the baby — he's come from Germany to look at the baby? He hasn't looked at it yet. I don't think he knows we've got one . . . thinks I'm wheeling an empty pram around. I'm wondering sometimes. Can't you get him out of here?

ALOIS. We are going for a walk today. . . . It is Sunday — it is a walking day. I showed him the baby — he expressed great interest.

BRIDGET. What happened? Did his eyelids flutter? Don't show him my baby — I don't want the poor mite frightened.

ALOIS. You are talking about my brother. We are one family. Germany is one family. We will be great one day!

BRIDGET. Don't tell him that.

ALOIS. I will take him and show him to my German friends — Doctor Sphlitz — he is a philosopher. *(Goes to* ADOLF.*)* Adolf, we are going out now — walky time. And when we come home Bridget will have the supper — and get the room all clean and polished. Arise. Raus. *(*ADOLF *slowly stands up. Stands silently. Then starts to take the coat off.)* No we are going out.

BRIDGET. He thinks he's been out.

ALOIS. We come back for the supper — the roast beef — sliced thick — dah potato salad.

ADOLF. Yah. . . . *(He sits down.)*

BRIDGET. There won't be any supper, Adolf, till you've had a little wal-kies. . . . *(To* ALOIS*)* There's something wrong with his mind. You tell him something, he thinks he's done it . . . they get worse as they get older you know.

ALOIS.   What do you know of a man's exhaustion? *(To* ADOLF*)* Adolf, we are going to see all the buildings. We are going down to see the Liver . . . then we go to the docks and I will take you on the big ships. . . . *(makes gesture pulling cord and noise like ships fog horn.* ADOLF *stands up. Puts on coat.)* There you see. He is getting the message. Ve will speak German when we are amongst our friends.

BRIDGET.   I don't think you'll have any better luck — his mind is shut off — he's not with us at all. He should see a doctor. We can't afford that. . . .

ALOIS.   He will see Doctor Sphlitz. . . .

BRIDGET.   We'll have to take him to a real doctor tomorrow.

ALOIS.   Doctor Sphlitz is a real doctor . . . of philosophy.

BRIDGET.   Philosophy won't save him . . . he needs an injection. . . .

ADOLF.   We go now. . . . *(ALOIS looks delighted, as though a miracle has happened. Looks at* BRIDGET *as if to say 'I told you so.')*

ALOIS.   Now Adolf. If we get separated . . . you go up to a policeman . . . and you say . . . Stanhope Street — Toxteth Park . . . Stanhope Street — Toxteth Park. Now Adolf you say that. I am the policeman. You are lost — in Liverpool you are lost. . . .

ADOLF *stares at* ALOIS. *Then suddenly clutches his lapels. A slow smile comes across* ADOLF'S *face.*

ADOLF.   Stanhope Street — Toxteth Park. . .

ALOIS.   My God — I'll take you there myself. . ..

ADOLF *(grinning like an idiot).*   Stanhope Street — Toxteth Park.

BRIDGET.   Quick — get him our of here before he forgets it. . . .

ADOLF.   Stanhope Street — Toxteth Park. . . . *(ALOIS beckons to* ADOLF *and they exit.)* Stanhope Street — Toxteth Park. . . .

Scene 5

Christmas eve. The apartment. BRIDGET *and* ANNIE, *drinking tea.*

ANNIE.   Are they out then?

BRIDGET.   I hope so — I can still see him sitting there —

ANNIE.   Is he staying for Christmas like?

BRIDGET.   Looks like it. Oh aye. We'll have him for the New Year that's for sure. they won't have me much longer though. They're out to get a tree like. I said put some decorations on your Adolf — he'll do.

ANNIE.   Oh aye.

BRIDGET.   They've started talking politics.

ANNIE.   Oh I don't like that.

BRIDGET.   Nor do I. They want to resurrect a Greater Germany between 'em.

ANNIE.   How will they do that?

BRIDGET.   Did you put that cat out? I don't wan't him sleeping on top of the baby.

ANNIE.   Oh aye.

BRIDGET.   More tea luv.

ANNIE.   Ta luv. *(BRIDGET pours more tea.)* Your Alois is a handsome man, he shouldn't get tied up in politics.

BRIDGET.   Adolf's got an idea for a new currency. You cover the notes in cellophane. It stops 'em wearing out.

ANNIE.   Alright if you can get it.

BRIDGET.   Oh aye.

ANNIE.   I think I might be pregnant.

BRIDGET.   Oh aye . . . who's the lucky man.

ANNIE.   It might be Alois.

BRIDGET.   Oh aye . . . might be?

ANNIE.   He's been taking advantage of me lately.

BRIDGET.   Why didn't you stop him Annie?

ANNIE.   I didn't know how to. I thought I'd better talk to you about it.

BRIDGET.   You've left it a bit late.

ANNIE.   You've had a lot of experience handling him.

BRIDGET.   That's right.

ANNIE.   You told me he was a ladies man. You warned me right from word go.

BRIDGET.   Right. Don't you know how to defend yourself.

ANNIE.   No.

BRIDGET.   Don't you know how to reject a man's proposition?

ANNIE.   Oh I wouldn't like to do that. I don't get many

BRIDGET.   You're not bad looking Annie. How do you know it's Alois? It might be some of the others.

ANNIE.   Weren't no others. Not this time round.

BRIDGET.   Well it was your fault. I hope you enjoyed it.

ANNIE.   It was lovely . . . ta very much.

BRIDGET.   Don't mention it. Could you be more careful next time?

ANNIE.   I hope so.

BRIDGET.   You'll be looking for a husband then?

ANNIE.   I suppose I will.

BRIDGET.   How about Adolf? It would help him stay in the country.

ANNIE.   I don't mind.

BRIDGET.   You're not that simple are you?

ANNIE.   Well if it keeps it in the family I don't mind. Long as I can still see Alois, like.

BRIDGET.   I'm not sure about that. I'm not sure how that stands with my religion.

ANNIE.   Nor mine. Never mind.

BRIDGET.   I'm glad you told me.

ANNIE.   I'm glad I told yer.

BRIDGET.   If you married Adolf, our Adolf — do you think you could find somewhere to live? I wouldn't want you both on the settee. How far gone?

ANNIE.   Three months

BRIDGET.   That's six weeks over for Adolf. I mean if you got him to bed you'd have a lot of explaining to do. You were already six weeks gone when he arrived.

ANNIE.   Time flies.

BRIDGET. It certainly does.

ANNIE. I'm not too worried about it.

BRIDGET. Oh that's good. I said you were simple.

ANNIE. It'll all come out in the wash. It was worth it. You must know that. I didn't want to upset you — I didn't know who else to turn to, like.

BRIDGET. You don't want an abortion then?

ANNIE. Oh no — that's — that's against my religion.

BRIDGET. I could be annoyed about this Annie.

ANNIE. I know. I didn't know how to stop him. Not once he started like . . . he's a handsome man . . . he could do well in politics.

BRIDGET. I know.

ANNIE. Oh aye. How's he getting on with the safety razor?

BRIDGET. You want a man who can keep you. How about Doctor Sphlitz?

ANNIE. Oh no — he's too old for me. I don't mind Adolf . . . like I want someone I can fancy.

BRIDGET. You fancy him?

ANNIE. I don't mind at all. Does he bath?

BRIDGET. He had one.

ANNIE. That's alright then. Has he a trade?

BRIDGET. No . . . he's difficult.

ANNIE. Is he willing to learn one do you think?

BRIDGET. I don't think so. Would you go to America with him?

ANNIE. I don't think so. Not without Alois. I want us all to be together.

BRIDGET. It won't last — you know that.

ANNIE. While it lasts.

BRIDGET. I've got to make some long term plans for you.

ANNIE. Go ahead. I've got to be going now. Ta wack. *(ANNIE gets ready to leave. Kisses BRIDGET.)*

BRIDGET. Will you come by later for the carols?

ANNIE. I'd love to. . . Me mam'll be out. She's got a new man

BRIDGET. So have you. I'll bring you together don't worry. Mrs Adolf Hitler, eh?

ANNIE. I like the sound of that. Worrying don't help does it? Tara.

BRIDGET. Tara luv.

Scene 6

That evening. Round the Christmas tree. ALOIS, BRIDGET, ADOLF (sitting on settee), ANNIE, and DOCTOR SPHLITZ. They are singing 'Silent Night' in German. ANNIE sings a verse in English. They all join in with German verses again. ADOLF, staring out into space, sings with them. ALOIS serves drinks.

DOCTOR S. My dear Herr Hitler! This is a wonderful evening! Vunderstaun! Ve are gathered here to celebrate the emergence of the Greater Reich.

BRIDGET. To celebrate Christ's birthday.

DOCTOR S. Yah. That is so. He was not a Jew. I have it on good authority. He vos an Arab your Christ — descended from Ayrian stock.

BRIDGET. The Jews were Arabs once.

DOCTOR S. That is so. There are Arabs and Arabs. *(Shrugs.)* Vot does a woman know. They tend the fireside — and they bear the children — which will march into the future.

ALOIS.   There must be war. Don't you feel that Herr Doctor?

DOCTOR S.   With Japan? Yah. There will be a great European war — I am telling you that. And out of it will be forged a new greater Germany. *(ANNIE notices* ADOLF. *There are tears on his cheek.)*

ANNIE *(to* BRIDGET).   Adolf is crying.

ALOIS.   Why not? It is Christmas Eve. All good Germans cry.

DOCTOR S.   Yah.

ALOIS.   What is a celebration without tears.

ALOIS *gives* ANNIE'S *bottom a little squeeze.* BRIDGET *goes to* ADOLF. *Takes her hanky out, and wipes tears from his cheek.*

BRIDGET.   What's the matter, Adolf dear?

ADOLF *(pause).*   I . . . am . . . not mit family . . . for so long. . . .

BRIDGET.   Oh bless his heart. Fill his glass up someone. *(ALOIS bustles over.)*

ALOIS.   Yah yah. . . .

BRIDGET.   Everyone needs a family eh Adolf. Kin. Kinfold. *(ADOLF looks at* BRIDGET. *Doesn't answer.)* Time you settled down, Adolf.

DOCTOR S.   The great master race must emerge. I am saying that the German race has the historical role! To play in the emerging Europe. For we are not a nation of shopkeepers. We are descended from the Vikings. We are warriors!

BRIDGET.   Christmas is a time for peace.

DOCTOR S.   We are the pure stock. We must not intermarry with the Jew.

ALOIS.   I do not think that Adolf is understanding all you are saying.

DOCTOR S.   Eh? Adolf? Peace on earth! Good will to man! Yah! It is good to forge peace. The cost of Christ's blood brought us peace. And with blood we will forge the peace of the world. Under the superior races. Not the Americans, they are polyglot. *(To* BRIDGET*)* How is the baby Bridget? Were you knowing that the Irish Liverpool is descended from the Viking — who went to Spain — crossing to Cork — and intermarried with the Moor — who thank God came down through Africa — from the North — so that is alright. Your baby?

BRIDGET.   My baby's luvely.

DOCTOR S.   Your baby is of good stock. The German and the Liverpool Irish.

BRIDGET.   I don't worry about that.

DOCTOR S.   It is good to know. One day it will be good to know. I will vouch for you. *(Turning to* ADOLF*)* And Herr Adolf. He has expressed a passing interest in politics, which we will not discuss tonight. But we will need the artist in Germany. We will need the architect. . . . *(To* ALOIS*)* I vill not speak to him in German tonight — I know there is a house rule.

ALOIS.   We are learning to communicate as one big family.

DOCTOR S.   Good good — gut *(waving finger.)* Vy should not the German language be the master in this household?

ALOIS.   We are in Britain.

DOCTOR S.   All the more reasons for us to make where we are a part of the Greater Germany. We carry it in our hearts. *(Holds his heart.)* And in the language. Do not let the woman have the dominance with her tongue. They will not like it. If your wife's language rules in this household . . . but I will mind my own business. A Happy Christmas everyone.

ANNIE *starts singing 'I Saw Three Ships Come Sailing In'. Others join in — possibly with German verses.*

DOCTOR S.   Yah Yah! The German navy must be built up to be the equal of the British Fleet! The dominance of the seas is the vital factor for the next war! *(ADOLF stands up. DOCTOR SPHLITZ addresses his remarks to ADOLF.)* War you understand! It must come!

ADOLF.   Yah. . .

DOCTOR S.   Adolf! You are a young man. You do not understand these things! You understand poverty and deprivation! You are an artist! But the artists will flourish in the new Europe! He vill be protected! This you vill not bother your head about! You vill be designing your. . . . *(Hands flutter.)* The buildings! For the new Empire — which mark my words — will be Germanic!

ADOLF *(doesn't seem to understand).*   Yah?

DOCTOR S *(in German).*   Germany will be great!

ADOLF.   Yah. *(Clears his throat.)*

Then ADOLF starts singing a German carol. It is rather sweet one. They all join in.

Scene 7

Later that evening. ADOLF sits at one end of the settee, and ANNIE the other. ALOIS and BRIDGET come through from rear, BRIDGET putting on gloves. ANNIE is dressed ready to go to mass.

BRIDGET.   We're going to mass now. Are you coming?

ALOIS.   No I will stay with Adolf.

BRIDGET.   You can both come. You don't have to join in. It's a beautiful ceremony, that's all — you can take it that way.

ALOIS.   No — you go. Someone must stay with the baby.

BRIDGET.   I don't care about the baby. You men — you think you can treat us like animals — for rearing your young soldiers. Don't you think we're people in our own right? Me and Annie? Do you really think we're an appendage to your masculine world? Do you really think you can slot us into your system of thought? You and Doctor Sphlitz? Why don't you go ahead and get the baby farms going? I thought you were a good person.

ALOIS.   Shh . . . not now. *(ANNIE stands.)*

ANNIE.   I'll get my gloves. It's been a lovely evening. I'll meet you downstairs.

BRIDGET.   Alright Annie.

ANNIE.   Goodnight Herr Adolf. Thank you for your company. I found it most pleasant. *(ADOLF. stares at her. Stands. Bows.)*

ADOLF.   Gute Nacht. *(ANNIE exits. ADOLF sits down again.)*

ALOIS.   Yes, you run along. Your religion is a great consolation.

BRIDGET.   I don't want consolation. I want a good life. I want to know somebody. I think we're strangers.

ALOIS.   We have lots of fun together. Now we are categorizing each other. We are expecting things from each other. When we were strangers — then we were intimate. That's how it goes.

BRIDGET. I know about you and Annie.

ALOIS. So? What do you know?

BRIDGET. You made her pregnant haven't you? You put her in the puddin' club. I don't mind — it seems so pointless that's all. I mean it's another thing we've got to cope with isn't it? Have you ever looked at it that way? I mean your system of thought — it's creating chaos. Do you know what you're doing?

ALOIS. I must live. You have known what sort of a man I am. I have left another woman to come to you.

BRIDGET. I'm not trying to change you. *(She kisses him lightly.)* I am saying we must do something about it. Why should I expect you to behave different just 'cos you married me. You were formed in character long before I met you. The only thing's going to stop you is exhaustion — old age.

ALOIS. I do not believe in old age — it is a superstition.

BRIDGET. Well what are you going to do about all the offspring you're bringing into the world? Someone's got to look after them. I mean do you want to leave me for her?

ALOIS. No I have no such plan. I . . . I want to breathe . . . I . . . live. . . .

BRIDGET. That others may die.

ALOIS. I am not killing anybody. I have always resisted the draft — with my two feet. I am for life.

ANNIE *(off)*. Are you coming! Bridget!

ALOIS. I speak of war as a historical necessity . . . that is all. My stomach is aching with this news.

ANNIE *(off)*. Bridget!

BRIDGET *(Calls softly so as not to wake the baby)*. Coming. . . . *(To* ALOIS*)* Well — she's interested in your brother, if we can get him looking presentable.

ALOIS. That is a good idea.

BRIDGET. Aren't you playing God?

ALOIS. I hope not. I hope I am expressing — the life force. It will not be denied. For He has made us and not we ourselves.

BRIDGET. Speak to your brother. Let's hope it all comes out in the wash.

ALOIS. I hope . . . I hope so. Bridget. . . .

BRIDGET. I only want a laugh, a few laughs. But how can we make it work that way?

ALOIS. It will work. Go now. *(*BRIDGET *exits.* ALOIS *goes to audience.)*

ALOIS. The following conversation took place in German. *(*ALOIS *sits beside his brother)* We have had a good evening Adolf.

ADOLF. Yah.

ALOIS. I am a man. And I have done what a man may do under his own roof. That is, Adolf, I have expressed myself, as Byron would have done. Do you get my meaning? A man must soar into the clouds, beyond morality — bourgeois morality. If I say I have done wrong — then I say to live is wrong. I am saying (*opens his hands*) I have made Annie pregnant. Do you condemn me? me?

ADOLF. Nein.

ALOIS. Good. Do you approve?

ADOLF. Nein.

ALOIS. You who read so much? I am making you an offer, Adolf. Would you like to start a new life in England? Will you marry Annie for me? I will be eternally grateful.

ADOLF. This is no good for family life.

ALOIS. You do not have the family — I have the family. I know what is good for family life. To live is to invite disaster. I am telling you that.

ADOLF. There are higher courts will judge our actions. Destiny.

ALOIS. Yah destiny. Meanwhile will you marry her for fifty pound? And then you will be OK to stay in Britain.

ADOLF. Is she Jewish?

ALOIS. Nein.

ADOLF. Is there any strain of the Jew?

ALOIS. No more than in our family. You know our father, old Alois — God rest his soul — that he came from obscure origins.

ADOLF. That will not always be so. This marriage of convenience may not be convenient for me . . . without love.

ALOIS. I am suggesting that you love. There will be a courtship naturally — a brief courtship.

ADOLF. Without love.

ALOIS. You could love her — this is what I am suggesting.

ADOLF. To love her would be difficult under the circumstances.

ALOIS. Love is not always necessary in marriage. She is a good cook — Annie — a man needs a good cook behind him. And she is good round the house. Are not your ideas big enough to include this arrangement? Love may come later.

ADOLF. I do not believe in this sort of arrangement, Alois. If I grow to love her. . . .

ALOIS. Quickly please. Grow quickly to her love. . . .

ADOLF. If. . . .

ALOIS. She is very fond of you — already. And I want to make you a wedding gift.

ADOLF. You have already done that. . . .

ALOIS. Think of your life. What does it amount to — nothing. You can make one person happy. Me. You can make her happy. You have a chance to make something of your life. I am offering you a — a purpose. You are half dead when you come here. Now life is offering a big chance. A wife and family — think of that — fifty pound to buy a flat, yah? You are away — as an artist — I know many Germans who will hire you for portraits. It is a chance to be a family man. *(Puts his arm round him)* Look here — I have done the hard work for you. Are you. . . .

ADOLF. Yah. . . .

ALOIS. Well it is not so pleasant. But once things are going well. There are African tribes where the virginity is taken. This makes the marriage good. It is a matter of attitude, Adolf.

ADOLF. I . . . do not know whether this is my destiny. . . .

ALOIS. You haven't got a destiny. You have a life. Make it as comfortable for yourself as you can. I am offering you a good start. Why should you not love her? Who are you? She is a nice girl. I vouch for it. Would I be finished?

Yah . . . with her . . . yah. Fresh pastures. My wife loves me. I live — to breathe. I love. I love. I cannot help it. I am planting the good seed everywhere. Yah. *(Stands.)* Have a drink? You know Joseph married a virgin? That was an act of love. Why can't you do this for me?

ADOLF.   That is a Judaeo-Christian concept.

ALOIS.   I don't care what it is. I tell you that girl fancies you now. She is a live wire. She can make a man of you. Who are you to pick and choose? Life comes along and says 'Take me. . . .' Who are you?

ADOLF.   I don't know.

ALOIS.   You are nothing. You came to me nothing. I am making you something. This is your last chance. If you let go you will sink again. Marry her — join the Liverpool German colony. You will have good friends. No scandal. You are able to help me with the safety razor sales in London later. She is a good girl — think what it is like to lie beside a woman every night. She will never blame you — for your behaviour — for she will know what you have rescued her from. She is a good girl. She will be grateful — Annie — all her days. Think it over. *(ALOIS gives ADOLF drink.)* Cheers! Happy Christmas!

ADOLF.   Happy Christmas.

ALOIS.   Well, is to be? The comfort? The security? The love and affection that will surely grow?

ADOLF.   I don't know.

ALOIS.   Will you try? You have nothing else to do.

ADOLF.   I don't feel so well.

ALOIS.   That is why. You are a virgin. That is why. She will make you feel well. Give her a chance. I promise you I will never lay another finger on her. My friend — these arrangements are happening all over the world. This is the love of family life. Great happiness can come from such things. And a family — can be knit together. You call it the skeleton in the cupboard. I call it the skeleton upon which the family hang the flesh of their life. Will you do this for me? Will you do this for yourself? Will you court her?

ADOLF.   I will try — but I don't have much strength.

ALOIS.   Trying gives you the strength — what am I telling you. It will make you feel a beautiful man. And you don't have to worry, because she is ready. . . . Her family are away — that part of her family represented by her father — he is a seaman.

ADOLF.   How often does he. . . .

ALOIS.   Come home yah? No he does not come home. And the mother is loose I am telling you. But apart from that it is a very good family. . . . *(Firmly)* It is what you make of it, Adolf. She is a woman — you are a man. She is good to lie with. She is experienced now. And that will help you because you need that. I have — done that for you. I am telling you about life — not dreams. Never be ashamed to live. I am offering you an opportunity. Destiny has brought you here! With that money. I don't mind. Why did you come? Because you felt impelled? Vy did the money arrive just in time? So you had to leave the country? Why did you have to leave the country just then? History makes its own decisions, Adolf. Do not fight your destiny. Marry Annie. And have a good family life.

ADOLF.   I will . . . consider it.

ACT TWO

Scene 1

BARON VON MINSKIN'S *studio.* BARON VON MINSKIN *in a wheelchair, is wheeled in by his* VALET. *Followed by* DOCTOR SPHLITZ. VALET *bows and retires.*

BARON.   And you tell me you have an artist who will do these pictures for us?
DOCTOR S.   Yah, your excellency — that is so.
BARON.   That is good. I will not pay much.
DOCTOR S.   Not much is a fortune to this fellow.
BARON.   Does he know the task?
DOCTOR S.   He does not know in so many words. How can words describe what your Excellency required?
BARON.   For my portrait of pornography he has not been told that he will model?
DOCTOR S.   He is the painter.
BARON.   Jawohl, and he will model as well, I tell you. I will not pay out twice for one job. It will be self-portrait, yah? We have the long mirror here. This portrait will be of the destitute workman masturbating. I vish to send it to Kaiser Vilhelm. I want it just like the real thing. You understand that?
DOCTOR S.   Jawohl. These vorkmen have not the strength to masturbate.
BARON.   It is by masturbating they have lost their strength. How is it that they grope their way round the streets but through the excess of masturbation. I want to captivate that corruption of the vorking man.
DOCTOR S.   Jawohl — we have the subject for you — and he will do a good self-portrait. He is from the streets of Vienna where he nearly died.
BARON.   Of masturbation? It must be documented.
DOCTOR S.   He is outside at the moment, waiting for you.
BARON.   Quick. I hope you have not left him alone.
DOCTOR S.   No, he is with his brother. . . .
BARON.   Thank God.
DOCTOR S.   He knows only that you are the Prince of the German art colony. He is anxious to meet you. . . . He did not know that in Liverpool we have such an enclave. . . .
BARON.   Where the business is — there are the good Germans.
DOCTOR S.   Jawohl.
BARON.   This portrait will be entitled 'British Working Class Unemployed Person Masturbating On the Clyde'.
DOCTOR S.   Yah. The Clyde is not in Liverpool.
BARON.   That does not matter. It sounds very good. These are the preparations for war which we are making. We are making a good point.
DOCTOR S.   Does it matter that the workman who is destitute and unemployed is German?
BARON *(considers this).*   As long as he can masturbate, I don't mind. Show him in now — while he has some strength.

DOCTOR *exits. Brings back* ADOLF.

DOCTOR S *(calls off)*.   Herr Alois — if you will wait please.

ADOLF *carries easel and painting materials. He clicks his heels, and bows to* BARON.

BARON.   Young man — you may commence.

DOCTOR S.   This is Herr Adolf Hitler. . . .

BARON.   I don't care who he is. He can remove his clothes and start his self portrait now. *(ADOLF looks mystified.)*

DOCTOR S.   The Baron wishes you to do a self-portrait in the long mirror. He will pay you twenty pound. It must be nude — masturbating. . . . The Baron will be watching while you do this — your brush work. Me — I want no commission. I am to explain that this is pornography of the highest order and vill be used as propoganda against the British. This will open many doors for you Adolf. Not as the masturbating painter. You can work work your way up to portraits of fine ladies. *(To BARON)* Yah?

BARON.   Yah. You will paint my wife later. This is a private work.

DOCTOR S.   You may disguise your face. This is a man's work — we would not ask anyone. You have been picked Adolf, not for your skills alone, but for your body — to lend itself to the task in hand. All must be bent to the vill of the purpose which only the Baron in his wisdom knows.

BARON.   Do not be alarmed. Pornography has served to describe the decadence of the ages. This is a necessary picture for posterity. Only I can judge. Are you able to masturbate? Have you the strength?

DOCTOR S.   The Baron — His Excellency requires an answer. . . .

ADOLF.   It is not my destiny to masturbate for his Excellency. . . . *(ADOLF exits.)*

BARON.   So. . . We vill try Augustus John. Not worth doing it on the cheap. . . .

Scene 2

The apartment. Evening. ADOLF *sits on the couch.* ALOIS *is standing nearby.*

ALOIS.   Why did you throw the easel into the Mersey, Adolf? And all your equipment? You were so pleased to be going to the Baron. Things were falling well for you. What happened? I lent you the money for that equipment. An advance on the fifty pounds which I have promised you. What happened in there? In the studio — of the Baron?

ADOLF.   I did not like the look of his face. I am finished with art.

ALOIS.   His face? You are a strange one. He has started many a young man. His patrongage would have made you. . .

ADOLF.   My hatred will break him. One day. . . . He asked me to masturbate for him. The tone of his voice was such I wanted to obey him . . . to please him. Like my father. *(Shouts)* But I hate him and I will triumph! Over such a man. *(Tearfully)* Who has such authority over me? Only destiny from now on. I am free. I have always kept my honour. I am free for the maiden who represents German womanhood. . . .

ALOIS.   Where is she?

ADOLF.   In my dreams.

ALOIS.   You must come out of your dreams — and go with a woman quickly. A virgin man — a boy such as you attracts such experience. Don't cry Adolf you meant well.

ADOLF.   There is no place for me on this earth.

ALOIS.   There is. Come out of your dreams. Go to the woman who is meant for you. To save you from these ghosts.

ADOLF.   You are saying it was not real? My experience with the Baron?

ALOIS.   I am saying you are making your reality. But you must use what is at hand around you. You must fuse your dreams into the earth. You must lift the material. You must penetrate. . . .

ADOLF.   Only in my dreams am I master. If I bring my dreams to earth then I must master it. For in no foul corner will there reside any man to rule over me and tell me to masturbate!

Scene 3

The apartment. It is dark. ADOLF *is asleep on the couch. He cries out.* ALOIS *enters. Lights the gas bracket.*

ALOIS.   Adolf! *(ADOLF sits up.)*

ADOLF.   Were you in here? Did you lend me money to go to the Baron? To paint? Did I go to the studio?

ALOIS.   No. It is Christmas morning. It will be light soon . . . Would you like an early breakfast Adolf?

ADOLF *(stares at* ALOIS *to find the reality)*. Jawohl . . .

Scene 4

About a month later. The apartment. Evening. BRIDGET *and* ANNIE.

BRIDGET.   I think he'll propose tonight.

ANNIE.   Oh aye, who to?

BRIDGET.   You. Didn't you have any inkling?

ANNIE.   Well he's been looking at me funny lately.

BRIDGET.   That'll be it. You see he's had a language problem.

ANNIE.   Oh aye.

BRIDGET.   But he's coming on handsome, fattening up, smartening up.

ANNIE.   Oh I noticed.

BRIDGET.   And he's agreed, more or less. Hasn't he taken you on any of his walks.

ANNIE.   No, not to my knowledge.

BRIDGET.   Oh. He might have asked you. You might not have known it.

ANNIE.   He grabbed me arm once. It hurt.

BRIDGET.   Did he drag you towards the door.

ANNIE.   No, no he didn't drag me anywhere.

BRIDGET.   More's the pity.

ANNIE.   Aye . . . oh aye. I was ready.

BRIDGET.   He's been having trouble with the Baron. It's a recurring dream he
gets. I want to get him married — that should cure it — it'll be best all round.

ANNIE *(looking at her stomach)*.   It'll be best all round me. I had a proposal
from Doctor Sphlitz.

BRIDGET.   Oh — was it marriage?

ANNIE.   Might have been — hard to tell. He wanted me to move in.

BRIDGET.   Housekeeper?

ANNIE.   Might have been that.

BRIDGET.   You've got a tongue in your head, you know. You should use it. I
mean you can make it clear marriage is the only answer.

ANNIE.   I won't marry that old man — rather stick me head in the gas oven.
I'm hoping to marry Adolf.

BRIDGET.   Well you might have to say yes before he asks properly. I mean,
turn a half opportunity into something, won't you?

ANNIE.   Won't he do it proper?

BRIDGET.   What?

ANNIE.   Won't he ask me proper? I mean how will I know luv.

BRIDGET.   Well if he starts taking his trousers off — you pop the question.

ANNIE.   He won't do that, he's too much the gentleman. Our Adolf. He's
never been less than polite to me. And he knows about my position. He opens
doors for me. I'm not going anywhere half the time. Opened the broom cupboard he did last week — I don't know what he thinks I'd do in there.

BRIDGET.   You're onto a good thing. He obviously fancies yer. Next time
take him in the broom cupboard — anything — get on with it. We're going out
tonight Alois and me. We're going to give you every opportunity. When Alois
gets back from work we're going straight out. You're baby sitting see — and
you fix supper for both of yer.

ANNIE.   Where's Adolf?

BRIDGET.   Well he gets up about midday — which is really bright — has a bite
to eat — and goes for a walk along the docks. Every day the same. Down the
docks. He's weighing up the might of the British Navy. He's very impressed
with it. You see Germany's inland — mainly.

ANNIE.   Oh that's handy.

BRIDGET.   What?

ANNIE.   Well you can get everywhere walking.

BRIDGET.   I think he plans on that. He talks about Russia sometimes. He
says, well it's only a walk from Berlin to Moscow. *(Sound of ALOIS off.)*

ALOIS *(off)*.   Hello. Come on Adolf.

BRIDGET.   Sometimes Adolf meets him on the way home. Now you're looking nice tonight. This is your big night. (*Enter* ALOIS. *Followed by* ADOLF
carrying flowers.)

ALOIS.   Hello! Hello darling! *(He kisses his wife.)* Hello Annie.

ADOLF.   Good evening. . . .

He sits on the settee holding the flowers. Enter the BARON, *pushed by* VALET.
BARON *wears frock coat and top hat. He signals for* VALET *to retire.* VALET
exits. ADOLF *stands up on their entrance. No one else seems to notice.*

BRIDGET.   Well we're going out tonight for supper. We're seeing some actress friends of mine. Surprise, surprise.

ADOLF.   Please. Do not leave me.

BRIDGET.   It's alright, Annie will look after you. And give her those flowers Adolf. She'll put 'em in water, with an aspirin. *(ADOLF awkwardly hands ANNIE the flowers. The bunch is rather jaded.)*

ADOLF.   Please.

ANNIE.   Oh ta. What shall I do with 'em? Eat em?

BRIDGET.   No put 'em in a vase. Here give 'em to me. Sit down Annie — keep Adolf company. He looks like he's seen a ghost. Those long walks aren't doing him any good. *(She takes the flowers.)* The might of the British Navy is too much for him. Did you see any big ships today Adolf?

ADOLF.   Yah.

BRIDGET.   Well sit down. *(ADOLF sits down again at one end of the settee. ANNIE sits down, the other end, BRIDGET exits to kitchen.)* I'll get me hat.

ALOIS.   So we are seeing actresses tonight. *(Rubs hands)* Good. Good.

BRIDGET *(off).*   You keep your hands off 'em. You're in enough trouble.

ALOIS.   Yah.

BRIDGET.   He's all man *(She comes back with her hat. Fixes it in a mirror.)* Now luv. Your supper's in the oven, so don't go sticking your head in it. Have a nice night. We'll be back late. Very late. You hear that, Adolf. Late. Later than you think.

ADOLF.   Yah.

BRIDGET.   The baby's asleep — there's nothing to worry about — so just enjoy yourselves. Don't make too much noise. Can't you sit closer than that. . . . Well have fun. *(ALOIS takes her arm.)*

ALOIS.   Come.

BRIDGET.   How do I look?

ALOIS.   Like the day I first met you. . . .

BRIDGET.   Oh do I? That's nice. Tara.

ALOIS.   Tara. . .

ADOLF stands up. ALOIS and BRIDGET exit. They sit in silence for a while. The BARON in his wheelchair — watching.

ADOLF.   Today there is the SS Margaret . . . just arrived from Singapore.

ANNIE.   Oh that's nice.

ADOLF.   Yah. It is very nice. . . . And today the SS Amelia leaves for Jamaica.

ANNIE.   Oh there's some nice girls names on those ships.

ADOLF.   Yah . . . I do not like.

ANNIE.   Eh?

ADOLF.   Any other girl. . . .

ANNIE.   Ohh. Oh that's nice. *(ANNIE moves a bit close.)*

ADOLF.   Bananas. . . . Yah. . . . *(ANNIE waits to be enlightened.)* To Jamaica bound for bananas yah?

ANNIE.   Oh yes — nothing like a nice banana.

ADOLF.   The MV Caernarvon Castle has arrived from South Africa — dock three.

ANNIE.   Oh.

ADOLF.   With a nice lot of passengers. . . .

ANNIE.   Oh that's good.

ADOLF.   Yah — they were a nice bunch. . . .

BARON. Get on with it.

ADOLF. What?

BARON. Masturbating. *(ADOLF stands up.)*

ADOLF. Excuse me.

ANNIE. Where are you going?

ADOLF. Excuse me?

ANNIE. Oh — are you going to the men's room?

ADOLF. Pardon? *(ADOLF exits.)*

ANNIE *(calls after him).* I'll get the supper in. You must be starving after all the looking at those ships. I know I would.

ANNIE *goes to kitchen. Returns with tray. Lays up small table in front of couch. Goes back to kitchen. ADOLF comes back.*

BARON. You filthy swine! Hands down the seam of your trousers! *(ADOLF puts his hands down seams of trousers. Enter ANNIE with casserole.)*

ANNIE. Sit down then, Adolf. What are you standing there for? *(They sit down and ANNIE serves the meal.)*

ANNIE. I cook aswell.

ADOLF. Yah.

ANNIE. I'm a good cook. And I'm good round the house like. . . And I've got a nice personality. Well I think so. That is, I'm easy going. I don't pick on a man, if you know what I mean. . . . You can come and go as you please. . . .

ADOLF. Yah. Very good dinner. *(They eat.)*

ANNIE. What are your prospects?

ADOLF. Yah?

ANNIE. What are you planning to do like?

ADOLF *(doubtfully).* Yah . . . I am enjoying my dinner. Thank you. *(ANNIE nods.)* Yah thank you very much. It is a good dinner. *(Eats)* You. . . You are a good cook also? *(He stares at ANNIE. He seems to go rigid.)*

ANNIE. What's the matter luv? *(Looks at him searchingly.)* Are you. . . . Crying again are you? Come 'ere. . . . *(She puts her arm round him. Holds him to her.)*

BARON. No! That's enough! That's disgusting! Alphonse! *(VALET enters. BARON shakes fist at ADOLF.)* You have not heard the last of this!

ADOLF *(To BARON — as he sits up, pushing ANNIE back).* Go away.

BARON. This will mean a court martial. *(BARON exits, pushed by VALET.)*

ANNIE *(only hearing ADOLF).* What's the matter luv? You want me to go away? What have I done?

ADOLF *(turns to her).* You will marry me?

ANNIE. Oh yes certainly — please — thank you. . . . *(ADOLF goes down on his knees.)*

ADOLF. Annie. I now pronounce you my fiancée.

ANNIE. Well get up. Let's make the best of it. *(ADOLF gets up.)*

ADOLF. I know that you are with child. That's alright by me.

ANNIE. Bless you. Thank you. I'll cook you some lovely dinners. I'm no good but I'll do my best by you. I'll be eternally grateful. And if you want to watch the ships every night, just go down there — I'll understand.

ADOLF. You will kiss me, yah.

ANNIE. Oh yes.

ADOLF *(takes out miniature)*.   This . . . is my mother's picture.

ANNIE.   Oh she's lovely.

ADOLF.   She is . . dead.

ANNIE.   Oh you poor thing.

ADOLF *(suddenly)*.   It was the Jews.

ANNIE.   How can that be?

ADOLF.   It was not a German disease. There was a house with no windows. That is what she went into. She told me. And the Baron was there. It was dreadful.

ANNIE.   Yes.

ADOLF.   I am mopping her brow. And the baron is in there. And she is telling me . . . she is going in there to the Baron. Yah? It was a tower. That is what she told me. And then. She died, but I am thinking . . . the Baron is a nice man. For she looked so happy. Yah? And now I hope that this Baron will let my mother go. For he is a terrible man. And she went to him so happily. . . . Yah. And I want to be with her. To get her out of the tower. *(He stands up.)* To get her out of the tower!

BARON *enters, wheeled by* VALET.

BARON.   Then you must masturbate.

ADOLF *(to* ANNIE).   Excuse me.

ANNIE.   Where are you going, Adolf. Come back. You've just been. *(She grabs him.)* You're not going anywhere luv. You've not been well. Now lie down. *(ADOLF is crying.)*

ADOLF.   He will not let her go. . .

ANNIE.   Yes he will. *(ANNIE takes* ADOLF'S *trousers off.)*

ADOLF.   No.

ANNIE.   Yes. Yes.

ADOLF.   Ohhh no. . .

BARON.   Masturbate. . .

ANNIE *lies on couch with him. Pulls up blanket over them.*

ANNIE.   Now just be still luv. You'll be alright. Let me do the work. I can help you. . . .

ADOLF.   Don't.

ANNIE.   Yes.

ADOLF.   Touch. . . .

ANNIE.   Yes. . . .

BARON *suddenly yells.* VALET *tips him out of the wheelchair. Kicks* BARON. ADOLF *watches, over* ANNIE'S *shoulder.* VALET *exits with wheelchair.*

ANNIE.   There . . . there . . . (BARON *crawls out — moaning.)*

ADOLF.   Mutter.

ANNIE *(softly)*.   She's alright . . .

ADOLF.   Yahh . . .

Scene 5

The next morning. The apartment. ADOLF *asleep on the settee.* ALOIS *in dressing gown, tiptoes in. Goes off, fetches milk.* ADOLF *wakes, sits bolt upright.*

ALOIS.   There you are you rascal. We came in late. You were not alone. She must have left after three o'clock this morning. Well now. How does it feel to be a man?

ADOLF.   You make a cup of tea?

Scene 6

The streets of Liverpool. Snow. Enter ADOLF, *done up in his brother's over-coat. He is waiting for someone. Enter* TRAMP *playing clarinet, begging. There are a few passers-by.* ADOLF *jumps up and down to keep warm. This turns into a dance, admidst the snow flakes. Passers-by stop and watch. Enter* ANNIE. *She sees* ADOLF. *Goes up to him. He takes her hand and gets her to join in the dance. As passers-by throw coins into the* TRAMP'S *hat,* ADOLF *and* ANNIE *run off — laughing. Scene changes to docks. The snow has stopped. Sound of ships' sirens — coming over the Mersey — muffled. They stop and brush snow from their coats. They kiss.*

ANNIE.   Oh Adolf — I am so happy. I've seen a nice little flat — down the road from your brother's.

ADOLF.   Yah. It is good. . . .

ANNIE.   How will we live?

ADOLF.   How do the sparrows live?

ANNIE.   You've got the money?

ADOLF.   Yah — for deposit one year. . . . *(Turns and looks over the water.)* What is the might of this sea power? Where is this Great Britain? What does it mean? That will-power has built an empire. And yet man stands still with his heart in his pocket. *(Turns to* ANNIE.*)* This night I dare not touch, for if I describe it — it will surely go away. For once in my life I am at one with the world. And yet I have not conquered it. It is mine. There was nothing to con-quer. It was given me. . . . Come. . . . *(They walk away, hand in hand.)*

ANNIE *(points).*   Look at that snowman! Oh look at that hat! You must have it. . . . *(She runs off.)*

ADOLF.   A hat! *(She runs back, clutching an old hat. Sound of approaching horse-cab — rapid.)* Annie!

She is struck down. A few people gather round.

CROWD.   Ohh the poor thing! Where's the bastard that did it? *(The cab has disappeared.* ADOLF *stands — watching.)* Get her to the hospital! Right. Lift her gentle now. This way. Easy does it. Oh the poor kid. These bastards. Come out of the night. . . .

They carry her off.

FIRST STRANGER *(to* ADOLF*).*   Are you with her then?

ADOLF.   Nein. . . .
FIRST STRANGER.   Did you see how it happened?
ADOLF.   Nein. . . .
FIRST STRANGER.   Are you sure you don't know her lad? Can you tell us anything?

ADOLF *picks up the hat.* SECOND STRANGER *comes back.*

SECOND STRANGER.   She's a goner. Any witnesses?
FIRST STRANGER.   Only this fella. He was hanging around. Lovers' tiff, do you think? Pushed her under a passing cab. . . . Where's the police?
SECOND STRANGER.   They don't come down this far, not usually. They're bringing one now. *(To* ADOLF*)* Hey! You! You 'ang on son. They'll be wanting to question you. . . .

ADOLF *runs off. He enters another part of the stage. Bumps into* BARON, *muffled up against the cold, pushed by* VALET *in the wheelchair.*

BARON.   Masturbate. *(*ADOLF *recoils.)* You have seen the world. Now you must conquer it. It is the only way you will get it back. . . . *(To* VALET*)* Home Alphonse!

BARON *and* VALET *exit.* ADOLF *clutches the hat. He forces his hands up and pushed the hat onto his head.*

Scene 7

The apartment. The next morning. A POLICEMAN *and the* INSPECTOR.
ALOIS *and* BRIDGET. ADOLF *sitting on the settee.*

INSPECTOR.   This man ran away from the scene of the crime.
ALOIS.   There was no crime. You have not brought charges.
INSPECTOR.   Then why did he run? What was he running from? He does not deny that he was with the deceased, not any more.
ALOIS.   He has no reason to deny it. He ran because he was scared. He is an alien. He does not understand.
INSPECTOR.   Does he understand that the deceased Annie Watkins was pregnant? Does he understand that? By some four months.
ALOIS.   Vell there you are, you see. Adolf has only been here. . . .
INSPECTOR.   Adolf?
ALOIS.   That is a family name. Edmund. . . .
INSPECTOR *(to* ADOLF*).*   You are Edmund Hitler?
ADOLF.   Yah.
ALOIS.   What I am telling you, inspector, is that Edmund — my brother — has only been here three months. So if she was pregnant four months it is not his doing. . . . Yah.
INSPECTOR.   Then whose doing was it?
ALOIS.   Well, I don't know.
INSPECTOR.   He was going to marry a girl who was pregnant by another man?
BRIDGET.   Can't you leave off, can't you? What business is it of yours?

INSPECTOR.   We suspect. . . .

BRIDGET.   Suspect what you like! Why don't you get out of here! Why doesn't he go? He's not making things any better.

INSPECTOR.   If Herr Edmund Hitler is engaged to be married to a girl who is pregnant by another man and he discovers this. . . . *(ADOLF stands up.)*

ADOLF.   I know . . . I know that she is pregnant.

INSPECTOR.   Getting someone else to do your dirty work, eh?

BRIDGET.   You're disgusting.

INSPECTOR.   You find out she's pregnant right? You're annoyed and push her under the cab. Naturally. It happens every day.

ADOLF.   Nein . . . I . . . love her. . . .

INSPECTOR.   What's love got to do with it?

ADOLF.   Nothing. . . . *(He sits down again.)*

INSPECTOR.   Was he marrying her to obtain status to stay in Great Britain.

BRIDGET.   Look, you haven't got anything on Adolf. Get out of here. Go on! Get out! We've got family grief! This is our business. Let us pick up the pieces will yer . . .

INSPECTOR.   I know you are grieved madam. If there is a crime we have to ascertain this.

BRIDGET.   If? If? If? That's an improvement. The scene of the accident we'll call it shall we. I know these two. I know Annie. They were in love. You won't find it in your manuals.

INSPECTOR.   A *crime passionel.* That's how it happens. Most of the time . . . jealousy . . . family affair. Yes . . . cover up eh. Very well. *(Closes notebook.)* I shan't waste more time on this. We can't prove anything. . . . *(To* ADOLF*)* You're not wanted in this country. Get out. . . . *(To* ALOIS*)* And we're not keen on you. Why don't you go back to hunland the lot of you. *(To* BRID-GET*)* You married him. Why don't you go back to the Fatherland with him? You're joined with him now. It's your choice.

BRIDGET.   I shall live where I want. With who I want. He's my husband. Now get out you filthy tyke.

INSPECTOR.   We'll get you the next time. It's the foreigners is causing the decay, of this country. Next time we'll get you. . . . Good day Ma'am. Good day sir.

INSPECTOR *and* POLICEMAN *exit.*

BRIDGET.   I'll make a cup of tea. That's the last thing we needed, that. . . . *(*BRIDGET *exits to kitchen.)*

ALOIS.   Adolf. This has been a blow. Of course I believe you. . . . You would not have second thoughts. You would not act in such a manner . . . would you? I ask you . . . brother to brother . . . did you kill her? Did you change your mind? Were you overcome with disgust? Did you push her perhaps? Not meaning she should go under the wheels? Were you ashamed that I . . . I did it to her? Was it too much for you?

ADOLF *gets up. Takes* ALOIS *by the collar.*

ADOLF.   Schweinhund! *(*ADOLF *pushes* ALOIS *away. He walks out of scene.)* Now I have only my destiny. . . . *(Enter* BARON *in wheelchair pushed by* VALET.*)* What has happened to me is good. It is a warning. . . .

People. There is a world that we will make. Without sentiment . . . bourgeois afflictions. I am chosen to be your leader, for fate will allow nothing else for me. I have sacrificed my life that a greater Germany will arise. I have stripped myself of all personal obligation. I am nothing except my determination, my will, my destiny that shall be married to the power of creating a new master race where sorrow cannot enter, where joy and health are one, where the new Wundervolk will play on the meadows. I do not see this world around me. We must destroy to make way for the new creation. We must without pity rid ourselves of all foreign elements so that German motherhood will flourish in security and goodwill and beauty. (*Cries out*) Mother!

Scene 8

The apartment. Later that morning. Enter DOCTOR SPHLITZ, *shown in by* ALOIS.

DOCTOR S.   Yah. Good evening. I find you at home. Good. The home is where the German repels all evil. Only good flourishes in the bosom of the family. Which brings me to my business. May I sit down?

ALOIS.   If you are staying.

DOCTOR S.   That is my intention. I would not be sitting down if I was going. I would be standing up. But first I would be sitting down.

ALOIS.   If you are sitting down because you have to stand up to go then by all means sit down — and stand up — and go.

DOCTOR S.   Are you telling me that I am calling at the wrong time?

ALOIS.   I am telling you that I am no longer German. (SPHLITZ *looks uncomprehending.*) That is German as opposed to Jewish. I am German distinctly because I was born in a certain place, which had to be somewhere if I am going to be born at all. I am German for the purposes of war. To fight. To join in arms, nation against nation. For that purpose nationality is intended. To get away from health and home and the good influence — which will kill all of us. Whereas in war — some survive — and they know they survive. But in peace how many know they are dead?

DOCTOR S.   I am not calling at a good time.

ALOIS.   You are calling at the best time. Which will never be good — for you. The good time for calling is over for you. Any time was good. But that is all past.

DOCTOR S.   I have not come here to be insulted Herr Hitler.

ALOIS.   In that case there is no point you coming here any more. You will go to the Germany colony.

DOCTOR S.   We are all part of the German colony.

ALOIS.   I am not part of the German colony. I am . . . what I am. . . . (ADOLF *enters unobserved.*)

DOCTOR S.   Yah. (*Laughs.*) You are a good German. And today you have a bad digestion. I will improve this. I will pay for your brother's fare home to Germany. I have the money here. . . .

ADOLF.   I will take it.

DOCTOR S (*still holding money*).   There are no conditions. The Fatherland deserves the best of the young. You will go alone of course.

ADOLF. Alone?

DOCTOR S. Without Annie.

ADOLF. Yah. Agreed. *(ADOLF takes the money.)*

DOCTOR S. And you will go immediately?

ADOLF. Nein.

DOCTOR S. Yah. I do not wish you to see Annie. There is work for you to do in the Fatherland. A young girl is not for you. She will work for me. Under my roof.

ADOLF. I do not think so.

DOCTOR S. What do you know, young man, of the power of the gentleman? With the years which make his attraction . . . the education. The learning, which can dazzle a young girl. I will teach her everything.

ADOLF. You are too late.

DOCTOR S. Too late? I will decide. How too late? I will reform her and make good use of her.

ADOLF. I doubt it.

DOCTOR S. You will go out of my way. That is all. You will go back to Germany. Alone. And I will give you twenty pounds. More. Leave everything to me. Go.

ADOLF. You will on no account ask for this money back?

DOCTOR S. Not if you keep your part of the bargain.

ADOLF *(takes twenty pounds)*. I will keep mine. Your stomach is too big. You are gross. And smell and sweat. I tell you Herr Doctor Sphlitz. She will not look at you dead.

DOCTOR S. That is my problem.

ADOLF. Yah.

ADOLF *holds out his hand with a wolfish grin. Grimly* SPHLITZ *shakes his hand.* SPHLITZ *exits.* ADOLF *clutches his stomach. We cannot tell whether he will laugh or cry. He does neither, but seems to be in intense physical pain.*

ADOLF. Yah yah yah. . . .

ALOIS. We are from the same seed Adolf. Our good father Alois.

ADOLF. I thank God we have different mothers. Were I from the same womb as yourself I would tear the bowels of this earth to get inside again and cut my way out through the flesh in bloody protest against my own conception.

ALOIS. All women are whores. They are all the same. I like whores. I love them. I reduce all women to that level — prostitute. And on that level I adore them. They are playthings. It is all a game. And you pay to play.

ADOLF. Would you speak of your own wife in such manner?

ALOIS. Yes. Marriage is the arrangement of the prostitute made in the market. A sale takes place . . . a contract . . . business. It is business as usual. But I do not hate them for it. Women. Women — Adolf. They are born into the market place. They must sell what they have to survive.

ADOLF. There are exceptions in German motherhood. There is that superior race which transcends the Jewish market. The market of the mind.

ALOIS. No Adolf. Confront life as it is. With its greed — its meaness — its lust in every human being and love them. We are all prostitutes and thieves. Do not look to the Jew for a scapegoat. Do not look to motherhood for a glorious example. You were born in lust and from that lust was forged a business contract — in law called marriage. Celebrated in white — a white wedding — and on white paper, in black ink, the contract. And black in death's garments shall only terminate that arrangement. This is the mockery of the market. It will happen to the Jew. it will happen to everyone. You are a child to look for scapegoats. And a child needs heroes. Populate your darkness. They are all ghosts. Only the light will dispel them. The truth.

Scene 9

Lime Street Station. STREET MUSICIANS.

MUSICIANS.   Hitler In Liverpool . . .
  You're such a fo-oo-ol.
  You came here one autumn day
  And now you must go away. . . .
  Education you got in this city.
  Education is never pretty.
  There's one thing that you got right,
  Our Navy is full of might,
  Our Isle is surrounded with water.
  We wish love had kept you and taught you,
  But Vienna was a harsher school
  Than our lovely Liverpool.
  Oh Hitler in Liverpool
  You're such a fool.
  You never saw the light on the Mersey.
  Annie never knitted you a jersey.
  Hitler in Liverpool. . . .

Scene 10

Lime Street Station. Enter ALOIS, BRIDGET, *and* ADOLF. *He clutches a small brown paper bag.*

BRIDGET.   Now you've got your sandwiches Adolf? Now you know you're always welcome, don't you? Not too soon luv. *(ALOIS takes ADOLF aside.)*
ALOIS.   Adolf, I have something for you. . . . *(gives him a leather box.)* You will find some addresses in that box — that will help you. If you will work, Adolf, you can be very big in Germany. . . . *(ADOLF opens box. Takes out a safety razor.)* Why don't you use it yourself? There are spare blades. . . . Show this instrument to who you will. When you get a reaction write to me. We will go into mass production — that is the future. . . Will you shake my hand? *(ADOLF does not take the extended hand. he gives ALOIS the box back, with the razor.)* How are you going to manage? What are you going back with now? How will you survive? I have given you a chance in life. . . . Well you must make your own chances. I'm not a bad chap. I am the black

sheep but I would have spared you misery Adolf. You came to us. I invited you to share our life. It is not my fault it did not work out. Sure we are not an ideal family, but we have life. Try to love us. . . . *(train noises.)*

BRIDGET *(approaching).*   It's platform three! We're late as usual. Goodbye Adolf. Catch that train. *(She hugs him.)* I must say you're looking better. You've put on a bit of weight. Never let yourself go like that again, will you. And don't worry about the fare luv. You've got enough on your plate. Find someone nice, some nice German girl. Don't read those books again . . . promise. . . . *(Whistles off.)* Tara.

ALOIS.   Bye bye Adolf. Till we meet again. . . .

ADOLF *(quietly).*   You will get everything that is coming to you. . . .

ADOLF *exits, through barrier,* ALOIS *and* BRIDGET *wave.* BARON *enters in wheelchair, pushed by* VALET. *They also have luggage. They go through the barrier. Sound of train. Whistles. Loud . . . then fading as train goes.*

Curtain

ONE ORANGE FOR THE BABY

Characters
HARRY
IVY
ANDREW
ALBERT
IAN
JENNY
RUTH
JANE
BABA
GALILEO
OSBORNE
PHIL
GIRLFRIEND
POSTMAN

First night at the Gate Theatre, London, 14th April 1980. Directed by John Antrobus. Designed by Phillippa Nash and Jim Daly.

IVY	Pam Merrick
HARRY	Carl Forgione
IAN	James Fleet
JEN	Lizza Aiken
ANDREW	Mike Burnside
ALBERT	Mike McKevitt
RUTH	Margaret Ashley
OSBORNE	Peter Stenson
BABA	Arthur Nightingale
JANE	Constance Reason
GALILEO	Brendan Murray
PHIL	Martin Kennedy
LORRAINE	Liz Stoll

ACT ONE

Scene 1

Early season. HARRY and IVY in old farmhouse kitchen. She lights a lamp as it gets dark outside.

HARRY. Ivy. Ivy . . . I confess.

IVY. You've already confessed.

HARRY. I confess again.

IVY. You confess every night.

HARRY. Only tonight I'd like to tell you a little more.

IVY. Go on.

HARRY. I enjoyed the third. I enjoyed the blonde . . . the long blonde hair parted . . . and her breath.

IVY. That's enough!

HARRY. Everything.

IVY. I'd rather know nothing. You started it.

HARRY. But you won't let it be finished.

IVY. Everything is finished . . . between us.

HARRY. Then me telling you more. . . .

IVY. Shut up.

HARRY. Cannot possibly make you angry as you have no feeling for me. Plump and moist, fair breasted. That is, the crest of her hair.

IVY. I'm going out.

HARRY. What?

IVY. Carry on.

HARRY. Where are you going?

IVY. For a walk.

HARRY. I'll come with you.

IVY. No, you have your memories. I have my future.

HARRY. You have no future.

IVY. Alright I have no future. I'll stay with you.

HARRY. Forever.

IVY. Forever.

HARRY. Forgive me.

IVY. Why should I?

HARRY. For your own sake.

IVY. I'm quite fond of you.

HARRY. It's not the same, you used to hate me.

IVY.   Yes.

HARRY.   There was passion and love.

IVY.   Your supper's ready.

HARRY.   Damm supper. Damn it. *(Skids plate off table and smashes it.)*

IVY.   You can do that as much as you like.

HARRY.   I'll set fire to the house tonight.

IVY.   Please yourself.

HARRY.   Ivy.

IVY.   I'm going out.

HARRY.   No you're not. I'll stop you.

IVY.   Then if you stop me I won't go out.

HARRY.   This is what you call passive resistance is it . . . you realize of course that I have stopped writing. The bills are piling up. Let them. It is deliberate. Economic sabotage. One day there will be no money for food . . . anything. And we will starve together.

IVY.   As you wish.

HARRY.   As I starve now.

IVY.   Harry.

HARRY.   Ivy

IVY.   What's the use?

HARRY.   I could leave you.

IVY.   I'll pack your bags.

HARRY.   You could leave me.

IVY.   Would you let me?

HARRY.   Not like this . . . not like this.

IVY.   Then I'll stay with you. We are married.

HARRY.   We are married, that is the point. Surely forgiveness. . . .

IVY.   The third, you say.

HARRY.   What?

IVY.   Stella.

HARRY.   Yes.

IVY.   Blond.

HARRY.   Yes.

IVY.   Plump.

HARRY.   Rather.

IVY.   Sure she wasn't six.

HARRY.   Number three.

IVY.   I forgive you.

HARRY.   Oh Ivy. . . .

IVY.   Now I'll go for a walk.

HARRY.   Alone.

IVY.   I'd rather.

HARRY.   With me?

IVY.   No.

HARRY.   What's the point . . . forgiveness . . . tonight?

IVY.   It doesn't make any difference. I can't. That's why I decided to forgive you. Because it doesn't make any difference.

HARRY.   Well what is the point of forgiveness?

IVY. Heaven knows.

HARRY. You are my wife. Once and for all you are my wife. I have rights . . . conjugal.

IVY. Take what you want. It won't make any difference to me.

HARRY. I'll hit you.

IVY. Hit me.

HARRY. I love you.

IVY. You've got your girlfriends for that.

HARRY. It's you I desire . . . my own wife.

IVY. You should have thought of that with number three, number two and number one. And number four and number five and number six. Any more?

HARRY. six.

Scene 2

Bar at a Country Club. Lights on. Early summer evening. Landlord is an ex-officer. It was an exciting thing to buy a pub after the war. But the war's been over a long time. His only customer at the moment is ALBERT.

ANDREW. And I took my dinner you see . . . yes.

ALBERT. Yes.

ANDREW. And I ate it.

ALBERT. In front of her.

ANDREW. In front of her . . . in front of her. I'll say in front of her.

ALBERT. What did she do?

ANDREW. She watched me. Every mouthful. In my own time.

ALBERT. And that night she left you.

ANDREW. That very night.

ALBERT. Do you think it was anything to do with the dinner.

ANDREW. God knows. Haggis. That's what it was, haggis. Every mouthful. I could feel her watching me.

ALBERT. Who did the washing up?

ANDREW. That plate, Albert, that plate has never been washed up. Would you like to see it.

ALBERT. Yes (ANDREW *brings out dirty plate* ALBERT *studies it.)*

ALBERT. If it had been me I'd have broken the bastard. *(Angrily)* Like that. *(Picks up plate and smashes it.)*

ANDREW. You've had too much to drink Albert.

ALBERT. I'm sorry.

ANDREW. Watch your language.

ALBERT. Yes.

ANDREW. You're a messy eater.

ALBERT. I know.

ANDREW. Don't eat pasties in front of my tourists. Don't expect to get served.

ALBERT. No I see. O.K. no haggis.

ANDREW. That's enough.

ALBERT. Heavens man.

ANDREW.   I know Albert.

IAN *enters. About twenty-eight. Jeans, trousers and jacket (Levis). Rucksack and sleeping-bag.*

IAN.   Pint and a pasty please. *(They look at him.* ANDREW *decides to serve him, though he's long-haired.)*
ANDREW.   A pint of ordinary?
IAN.   What's cheapest.
ANDREW.   Ordinary beer is cheapest. Director's beer is not.
IAN.   I'll have ordinary.
ANDREW.   You'll have ordinary.

ANDREW *serves him pint and pasty.* IAN *sips beer and bites pasty. They watch him chew his first mouthful. He is aware of them watching.*

ANDREW.   Done any fishing lately?
ALBERT.   Not for five years.
ANDREW.   They don't bite like they used to.
ALBERT.   They used to bite.
ANDREW.   They don't bite like they did.

They stare at IAN *chewing his pasty.*

IAN.   Got any mustard?
ANDREW.   Yes we have mustard. *(He doesn't give him any.)*
IAN.   Can I have some mustard?
ANDREW.   You would like some mustard.
IAN.   Yeah . . . please. *(*ANDREW *gives him some mustard.)*
ANDREW.   We had these prisoners of war.
ALBERT.   Oh yes.
ANDREW.   They were quite decent fellows and they treated us well.
ALBERT.   Germans?
ANDREW.   What?
ALBERT.   Were they Germans?
ANDREW.   Course they were Germans. What the bloody hell do you think they were, Chinese. We were in the middle of France.
ALBERT.   They could have been Italians.
ANDREW.   They weren't Italians they were Germans. They had some guts.
IAN.   We're all the same under the skin.
ANDREW.   I beg your pardon?
IAN.   The universal soldier. When I say jump, jump.

They watch him while he eats more pasty.

ANDREW.   India.
ALBERT.   Never been there.
ANDREW.   Nor have I. *(Leans across bar confidentially.)* You'll have to pay for that plate, you realize that?
ALBERT.   Of course.
IAN.   Any pads round here?
ANDREW.   I beg your pardon?
IAN.   Kipholes. I got a sleeping bag . . . need a floor.

ANDREW.   You are in need of a floor.

IAN.   Yeah.

ANDREW.   I see. Have you finished stirring the mustard?

IAN.   Sss . . . sure. Thank you.

IAN *gives* ANDREW *the mustard.* JENNY *enters. About twenty-three. Sleeping-bag and rucksack. She has been on the road,*

IAN.   Hi.

JENNY.   Where's my drink?

IAN.   I didn't know how long you'd be.

JENNY.   I'll have a pint.

IAN.   Yeah. The money . . . finito.

JENNY.   Wot?

IAN.   You want a bit of pasty?

JENNY.   That was my money. That was my money. That was my abortion
money you been spending.

IAN.   You . . . you're not having an abortion.

JENNY.   That money was given to me. To me . . . not you.

IAN.   Jen . . . you weren't pregnant.

JENNY.   That's not my fault. 'E din't give me that money for you to stuff yourself with pasties. *(From purse gives* IAN *coins.)* I'll have a brandy.

IAN.   Yeah . . . go ahead. Sure.

JENNY.   I financed this whole trip.

IAN.   It's not my fault your not pregnant.

JENNY.   I don't want to be pregnant.

IAN.   Well stop complaining. *(Goes to bar.)* Half of bitter.

JENNY.   A brandy.

IAN.   Yeah.

ANDREW.   You would like a brandy would you please thank you?

IAN.   That's it . . . do you want a pasty as well, do you Jen?

JENNY.   No thank you, I can't afford it.

IAN.   Mustard?

JENNY.   What's the good of mustard without a pasty?

IAN.   Don't get clever with me. I looked after you all the way down.

JENNY.   That's why it took three days. Keep seeing you come out the hedge
after I got the lift.

IAN.   You could have been molested. That driver . . . that mini . . . he had sex
maniac written all over him. My knees . . . my knees. I'm in front.

JENNY.   I'm sure you'll both be very happy. When you seeing him again?
(Takes brandy. Holds out hand for change.)

IAN *(hands change over).*   Pregnant . . . roll on . . . roll on.

JENNY.   I couldn't give him the money back. He went to a lot of trouble to get
it.

IAN.   Huh . . . fertility rites.

JENNY.   It meant a lot to him.

IAN.   I know, I know. Thinks he's the biggest puddin' man in the country now.
And me, what do I get? Not even a lousy brandy. Did you phone your sister?

JENNY.   I couldn't get a reply . . . the line's engaged.

IAN.   So you try again. We don't want to sleep in a field all night.

JENNY. I'm not sharing any more fields with you. *(Gets up. Takes her rucksack and sleeping-bag.)* You're like an animal.

IAN *(indicating her things)*. You can leave them.

JENNY. You're not reading my letters. Bastard.

IAN *(as* JENNY *exits)*. Thank you, thank you.

ANDREW *beckons to* IAN *with a finger.*

ANDREW. I do suggest that you and your young lady moderate your speech.

IAN. Yeah.

ANDREW. We've been through it as well, you know, we're not bloody idiots

IAN. The world is full of suffering.

ANDREW. What?

IAN. Sure. I know, I know. We got to suffer, right?

ANDREW. Be that as it may. You will be invited to drink up and leave if you don't pull yourself together.

HARRY *enters.*

HARRY. 'Evening.

ANDREW. Good evening Harry.

ALBERT. How do.

ANDREW. And what can we do for you?

HARRY. Shoot all the women. Large whisky please. Hello Albert. What do you think about 'em?

ALBERT. Aahh. . . .

HARRY. Been with one have you?

ALBERT. Aye . . . oh aye. Where to?

HARRY. Eh?

ALBERT. I been with me sister. To Penzance. That's enough for one year.

ANDREW. Now let's keep the conversation on an even keel shall we?

HARRY. They're monsters . . . monsters.

ANDREW. Are you referring to the gentler sex?

HARRY. Gentle! Bunch of bleedin' Christians. Blessed are the meek, they shall inherit the earth. They've done that.

ANDREW. Steady on. . . .

ALBERT. Women is alright.

HARRY. What?

ALBERT. Taken in small doses.

HARRY. What you talking about? How can you take a woman in small doses when you're married to her?

IAN. That . . . that's . . . *(they look at him)* interesting.

HARRY. What?

IAN. What you said about women.

HARRY. What did I say? I've forgotten.

IAN. About them being angels in disguise.

HARRY. I never said that.

IAN. No. I know. I mean my mother. She was the same.

HARRY. What?

IAN. Dad! *(They all look at him.)* He used to knock her around.

HARRY. Good . . . good for him.

ANDREW. Now then.

HARRY. They got the vote. What they want the railings as well.

IAN. He used to come home at night . . . after the war. . . .

ANDREW. The war. . . .

ALBERT. The war. . . .

ANDREW. We don't talk shop here. We don't talk about the war. . . .

ALBERT. Just 'cos you got an M.C.

ANDREW (chuckles). Alright, alright. What will you have Albert?

ALBERT. Pint of bitter please.

IAN. He hit her . . . and I . . . was angry. But I couldn't do anything. Then one day when I was older . . . I found him . . . crying in the gutter. What's up I said. Dad! What's the matter. I don't want to go home and hit her, he said. I don't want to go home and hit her. (ANDREW gives ALBERT beer.)

ANDREW. One pint . . . we'll put that up to charity.

ALBERT. Hole in the stocking. (Winks and drinks.)

HARRY. It's incredible. I mean here we are a balance of payments crisis and husbands hitting their wives. Nineteen thirty-three, that was all happening then. What's the good of a world war? It hasn't changed anything.

ANDREW. My God no.

HARRY. I don't agree.

ANDREW. What?

HARRY. We've got more communism.

ANDREW. Now don't start that. Harry . . . you've come here to drink, not convert us.

IAN. Yeah.

HARRY. What?

IAN. He was in the gutter and I helped him up. I took him home.

HARRY. What did he do?

IAN. Belted her.

HARRY. It's no answer.

IAN. No.

HARRY. What do you know? It might have been his answer. The war . . . oh . . . they were in it.

ANDREW. No. Not tonight.

HARRY. Yes you were . . . violence. You've been a violent man. Happiest days of your life. Then you come back. Land fit for heroes . . . and get fucked about by some women. You shouldn't have stopped. What Andrew? You should have come back home in the tank. Right outside her window. Are you there darling? I'm home. When she looks out . . . right let's get things straight.

ANDREW. He's off again.

IAN. That's very interesting.

HARRY. You weren't laughing.

IAN. No I found it interesting.

HARRY. Oh.

IAN. The war had a profound effect.

ANDREW. I'll say.

HARRY. Go on.

IAN. You know what I mean.

HARRY. No.

IAN.   Nothing . . . err nothing was the same . . . after.

HARRY.   What are you talking about?

IAN.   No . . . words I find difficult.

HARRY.   Well stop using them.

IAN.   Yeah.

HARRY.   Don't take me seriously

IAN.   I don't.

HARRY.   You're young . . . healthy.

IAN.   Yeah.

HARRY.   Ignorant.

IAN.   Well.

HARRY.   What the hell's it matter . . . intelligence? Where's it got me? I'm doing my nut.

IAN.   I think you've got to try.

HARRY.   What?

IAN.   To marry.

HARRY.   Go on.

IAN.   Health and ignorance. I mean and intelligence.

HARRY.   What's it matter . . . the war's not over. It never will be over. It's all right for these burkes. (*To* ANDREW) no offence. To rush and fight a few miserable henpecked German Fraus.

ALBERT.   What about the Jews?

HARRY.   What are we discussing, women or antisemitism?

IAN.   There must have been thousands.

HARRY.   What?

IAN.   Of Jews.

HARRY.   Oh Christ. *(To* ANDREW*)* 'Nother large scotch please. Do you want one?

IAN.   A pint please.

ANDREW.   Of ordinary.

HARRY.   Can't you feel the cats. . . .

IAN.   What?

HARRY.   The cats . . . the fur. Rising on their backs?

IAN.   Maybe. . . .

HARRY.   The fields . . . full . . . of grass. Women could be chewing. They don't have to be talking. Their breasts could fill. Don't talk to me about the bottle.

IAN.   This is very interesting.

HARRY.   Why?

IAN.   Look . . . look . . . my mother. I was breast fed.

HARRY.   How do you know?

IAN.   Well. . . .

HARRY.   Propaganda. Women won't ruin their tits on a kid . . . a brat. What you talking about? Cow and Gate, mate. Give 'em a night's sleep.

ALBERT.   Who?

HARRY.   All of 'em.

IAN.   That's what I'm after.

HARRY.   What?

IAN.   A floor.

Scene 3

Farm Kitchen. IVY *sits reading. Waiting for her husband to return from the pub. Door opens and* HARRY *comes in followed by* IAN.

HARRY. Put your sleeping bag down there. *(*IAN *just stands looking at* IVY*)* I said put your sleeping bag down. *(*IAN *doesn't. Just looks at* IVY.*)*

IVY. Who's this?

HARRY. I don't know. What's your name?

IAN. What? Ian.

HARRY. Put your sleeping bag down.

IAN. It is alright?

IVY. What?

HARRY *takes sleeping bag from* IAN *and puts it in corner.*

HARRY. He's got nowhere to sleep tonight.

IAN. I can sleep outside.

HARRY. What?

IAN. In the yard.

HARRY. It's still our property.

IAN. I mean it might be less . . . you know. . . .

HARRY. What's the good of walking two miles here just to sleep outside the door.

IAN. I know.

IVY. He might as well sleep here as you've brought him.

IAN. Thank you. I can be gone by the time you all wake up in the morning.

HARRY. How do you know?

IAN. Early.

HARRY. I get up early.

IAN. Oh . . . you know. . . .

IVY. Sit down.

IAN. Thank you. *(Sits down)* Can I have a cup of water please?

IVY. Would you like some tea?

IAN. No . . . don't bother.

IVY. I'll put the kettle on.

IAN. Well just hot water.

HARRY. What? You drink hot water?

IAN. I don't like it . . . but . . . but. . . .

IVY. I'll make some tea.

IAN. Thank you . . . no sugar.

IVY. What?

HARRY. He says he doesn't take sugar.

IAN. I do . . . sometimes . . . but . . . you know . . . it's extra . . . isn't it. . . .

IVY. What?

IAN. Trouble and expense.

HARRY. Well why not compromise. Have hot water with sugar and sleep standing up in the corner of the yard. Look, we're not hospitable.

IAN. I don't believe in compromise.

IVY. Oh Harry.

HARRY. What's he want?

IAN. Well. . . . Well you asked me out here.

IVY. If you've just asked him out here to insult him. . . . *(To* IAN*)* Don't worry . . . he gets like that.

IAN. I don't mind *(*IVY *goes out of room.)* Where's she gone?

HARRY. I don't know.

IAN. I just wondered.

HARRY. Did you. She's my wife.

IAN. Oh yeah . . . don't get me wrong. I'll go. *(Silence.)*

HARRY. She's attractive.

IAN. Yeah . . . in a funny kind of way.

HARRY. What?

IAN. Quiet.

HARRY. Quiet . . . quiet.

IAN. Can I go out in the yard?

HARRY. Yes. Are you coming back?

IAN. Yes.

IAN *goes into yard.* IVY *comes back.*

IVY. Where's he gone?

HARRY. In the yard. You're not complaining . . . you don't mind?

IVY. Anything you want.

HARRY. Sleep with him.

IVY. What?

HARRY. Go on. You're always so high and mighty. I'm always wrong. Sleep with him.

IVY. What, to please you?

IAN *knocks and comes back in.*

IAN. Sorry. . . .

HARRY. What?

IAN. I'm interrupting. *(Picks up his sleeping bag.)*

IVY. Are you going?

IAN. I don't mind.

IVY. It's silly. You've come all this way.

HARRY. He can go if he wants to.

IAN. Whatever you want.

HARRY. What?

IAN. You know . . . I don't want to cause any friction.

HARRY. Got quite an opinion of yourself.

IAN. What?

HARRY. Well one minute you're sleeping in the yard, next minute you imagine you can cause friction . . . come between husband and wife.

IVY. Harry.

IAN. I didn't say that.

IAN *puts his sleeping bag down again and starts rolling a cigarette. Kettle boils.*

IVY. You might as well have some tea. You can sleep in the kitchen . . . it's warm.

IAN. I'll have the tea.

HARRY. That's nice of you.

IVY. Are you going to be nice to him or can he go?

HARRY. I'm not being nasty to him. I can speak to someone can't I . . . in my own house? It's the way I have of speaking.

IAN. Yeah.

HARRY. Sit down Ian. *(IAN sits down.)* What do you travel round for?

IAN. Don't know.

HARRY. You are a traveller?

IAN. Yeah.

HARRY. Well is it the stress of civilisation?

IAN. That's it . . . and . . . and . . . you know. . . .

HARRY. What?

IAN. My dad. . . .

HARRY. Is he still alive?

IAN. He's dead . . . but this nutcase. . . .

HARRY. What?

IAN. This psychiatrist . . . you know, I went to see him . . . about my problem. . . .

HARRY. You've got a problem?

IAN. Yeah?

HARRY. Yeah . . . what is it?

IAN *(shakes his head).* It's . . . it's just a problem. Like . . . you know. . . .

HARRY. Crazy.

IAN. Everyone's got a problem. That's the way I look at it.

HARRY. But what is your problem?

IAN. My dad.

HARRY. But what about your dad?

IAN. I don't know. I left.

HARRY. Left?

IAN. This sick man . . . the cyclist. You know . . . he was hedging with me. I said what is the problem . . . my problem. Last time he burst into tears. I left.

HARRY. But he told you it was your dad.

IAN. It was one of these new places. You go in and the doctors are like you. He used to smear marmalade on the walls at breakfast time. Straight up. Try and get us at it. Therapy . . . yeah.

HARRY. Sounds interesting.

IAN. Yeah . . . he'd been there longer, see, than all of us.

HARRY. It was his living.

IVY. I wouldn't mind going there.

HARRY. Where?

IVY. Where I could lie around smearing marmalade on the walls all day.

IAN. We didn't do that.

IVY. Didn't you?

IAN. I read this book. A telephone directory. Straight up. For kicks . . . anti-art . . . a kind of serial. Some of these names. *(Shakes his head.)*

HARRY. Bit of a laugh.

IAN. Yeah . . . sometimes. Other times we'd cry. I read a name out it sounds silly. I came to this name and we cried.

IVY.   What was the name?

IAN.   Something like Polensky ... or something.

HARRY.   You find foreign names sad.

IAN.   Yeah. I mean ... what are they doing in an English directory?

IVY.   Just stuck there. Yes it's very sad.

HARRY.   I think it's a load of old cobblers

IVY *has made tea and they drink it.*

IVY.   What are you looking so depressed about?

HARRY.   Am I allowed to have a problem?

IVY.   If you like.

HARRY.   Bitch!

IAN.   I'll go after this.

IVY.   Stay. Harry wants you to. Don't you?

HARRY.   Yes. Yes I do. It's not often we have company. You must realize, Ian ... it's a big adjustment for us.

IAN.   Yeah.

HARRY.   Give us time.

IAN.   Oh yeah.

HARRY.   A third person ... a third person. I know it's only one night.

IAN.   I don't mind. *(*IVY *leaves the room.)* What's she keep leaving for?

HARRY.   Give us time to talk. I don't know.

IAN.   Yeah.

HARRY.   Do you find her attractive?

IAN.   Well she's a woman ... a woman, man.

HARRY.   I know. I know what a woman's like. I don't travel ... no sleeping-bag. But I do know what a woman's like.

IAN.   Yeah ... they're nice.

HARRY.   You think so. You make my neck ache.

IAN.   You want me to go.

HARRY.   Stay. You're a ... nice young man.

IAN.   Thank you.

HARRY.   She likes you.

IAN.   Yeah I'd say she did.

HARRY.   You can tell?

IAN.   Yeah. I mean. ...

HARRY.   Don't apologise.

IAN.   Have I said too much?

HARRY.   No.

IAN.   I just want to kip down.

HARRY.   I brought the subject up. *(Silence.)*

IAN.   I wonder where she's gone.

HARRY.   You seem very interested in her movements.

IAN.   I just wonder where she is.

HARRY.   You miss her.

IAN.   Come off it.

IVY *returns. Sits down and drinks her tea. Silence.* HARRY *abruptly gets up and goes out into the night, slamming the door behind him.*

IAN. Where's he gone?

IVY. I don't know.

IAN. Everyone keeps going out.

IVY. It's like that in this household. There's only two of us. We get on each other's nerves.

IAN. You got a problem. We all get problems. One day the big problem-maker will come and all will be solved. Yeah . . . yeah.

IVY. What is your problem?

IAN. My father. What is yours?

IVY. I haven't got one.

IAN. We've all got problems.

IVY. Harry is mine. I'm so cruel to him.

IAN. Be kind.

IVY. Eh?

IAN. Give the boy what he wants.

IVY. He seems to want something funny these days.

IAN. Yeah . . . funny. What's funny? It's all funny.

IVY. I mean more. . . .

IAN. Yeah.

IVY. I'm not sure that he does want it.

IAN. Give it to him.

IVY. It's not a matter of giving it to *him*.

IAN. Eh? *(HARRY comes back in abruptly.)*

HARRY. I could have heard everything you said.

IVY. Did you?

HARRY. No. Any secrets?

IAN. Excuse me?

IAN *goes out into the night leaving the door open.* HARRY *shuts it.*

HARRY. Go on then.

IVY. What?

HARRY. You're so pure aren't you. Smug. Passionless. Well do something about it. Soil yourself.

IVY. I shall do what I want.

HARRY. What do you want to do?

IVY. I don't know.

HARRY. Well do it . . . do it. Get it over with.

IVY. You're being silly. You've had too much to drink. *(She puts out a hand and touches him. He recoils.)*

HARRY. Do it. I want you to . . . I'm going mad.

Tap on the window. HARRY *goes and opens it. Outside* IAN.

IAN. Look.

HARRY. What?

IAN. Just . . . you know. Pass me out my sleeping-bag.

HARRY. You want to go?

IAN. It's raining.

HARRY. You want to stay?

IAN. Well . . . you know.

HARRY.   I don't know.
IVY.   What are you standing out there in the rain for?
IAN.   You know.
IVY.   Come in out of the rain.
IAN.   Well . . . it's not as easy as that. Can I have my tea please.

IVY *hands him tea through window. He stands outside in the rain drinking it.*

HARRY.   What's he doing?
IVY.   I don't care. You brought him here.
HARRY.   Are you coming in?
IAN.   If . . . if you really want me in.

HARRY *goes out through the door. Round to the window. Grabs* IAN *by the hand pulls him into room. Pushes him into a chair.*

IAN.   You want me to stay?
HARRY.   Yes.
IAN.   Because . . . like . . . I don't want to get up in the middle of the night. If I'm in . . . you know . . . I'm in.
HARRY.   You're in. *(He bolts the door.)* We're all in . . . we're all in . . . we're all in.

They look at each other. Fade lights. Then fade up again same scene. Clock strikes three.

IAN.   Three o'clock.
HARRY.   Two.
IAN.   Eh?
HARRY.   Two o'clock.
IAN.   You keep chimes time.
HARRY.   It's my house, Ian . . . I know what time it is.
IAN.   Yeah . . . sure. Don't get me wrong.

IVY *is asleep. Head in arms across the table. She stirs.*

IVY.   What's the time?
HARRY.   Three o'clock.
IVY.   Are we going to bed yet?
HARRY.   I'll say. I'll say when . . . bed . . . bed. The thought sickens me . . . frightens me. *(To* IAN*)* Do you like putting on pyjamas?
IAN.   I don't mind.
HARRY.   The thought sickens me. I can't put on pyjamas. Ask her. I can't put 'em on. It separates day and night so much . . . like some ghastly uniform. I sleep in my shirt.
IAN.   So do I.
HARRY.   Yes but out of. . . .
IAN.   Yeah.
HARRY.   Out of necessity.
IAN.   Yeah.
HARRY.   Out of fear . . . that's why I wear pyjamas.
IAN.   We all got a problem.
HARRY.   I have a pair.

IAN.   Yeah?

HARRY.   You can borrow.

IAN.   I'm indifferent.

HARRY.   Wear them.

IAN.   If you like. Can I have a bath? In the morning. *(HARRY stares at him.)* I don't want to interfere.

HARRY.   Sure . . . have one.

IAN.   Before I go . . . tell me . . . Harry. Some other fears. . . .

HARRY.   Every fear is a fatal attraction. That's why I'm frightened of death.

IAN.   You know what we should do. We should . . . yeah. . . . .

HARRY.   What?

IAN.   Read a directory. It's great gear . . . really. I only got as far as the E to K.

HARRY.   What about Polensky?

IAN.   What?

HARRY.   Where was Polensky?

IAN.   Croydon, I think. Purley. No Croydon. It was very funny.

HARRY.   Why wasn't Polensky under P?

IAN.   Why wasn't Polensky under P. Yeah. *(Laughs.)* Yeah . . . you see what I mean.

IVY.   Are we going to bed?

HARRY.   Go on up.

IVY.   I won't go without you. *(Puts hand out and touches HARRY.)*

HARRY.   Don't . . . don't play. I'm fed up of going to bed.

IVY.   I'm tired.

HARRY.   That's what you say. That's what everybody says. Bed . . . bed . . . bed is an evil place. Bed is a strange place . . . a troubled grave.

IAN.   I like that.

HARRY.   What?

IAN.   That troubled grave bit.

IVY.   I'm exhausted.

HARRY.   I don't trust you. I don't believe you are tired. It's circumstances . . . burn the house down. Would you be tired? Change a few factors . . . one factor.

IVY.   Oh come on. *(Puts hand out again. HARRY lets it rest on his arm.)*

IAN.   Don't mind me, Ivy.

IVY.   What?

IAN.   Don't mind me.

IVY.   I don't mind you, Ian.

HARRY *jumps up and goes out, slamming the door.*

IAN.   He's gone out again.

IVY.   He likes playing games. *(Yawns and stretches.)*

IAN.   I like the way you yawn. Yeah . . . I mean . . . no side. I just like it. It's great. It's a knockout. *(IVY rubs her eyes.)* I like the way you rub your eyes.

IVY.   It makes them bloodshot. I think I'll go on up . . . are you alright?

IAN.   Yes *(IVY stands up. IAN stands up.)*

IVY.   Are you tired?

IAN.   I don't know.

IVY.   You must be.

IAN. Do you think so.
IVY. Why are you so shy?
IAN. I'm not . . . everyone else is.
IVY. I'm not . . . every dog has his day.
IAN. Yeah. . . . *(He takes her hand)*
IVY. You've got a problem.
IAN. Yeah.
IVY. There's too many problems this time of night. This isn't the time for problems.
IAN. I know. *(They stand close together.)* I like Harry. You know . . . you know . . . he's mixed up. What does he want? *(Turns to door)* He's coming.
IVY. Goodnight.
IAN. I don't know.

IVY *exits.* HARRY *comes in front door. Shuts it behind him and locks up.*

HARRY. OK.
IAN. OK?
HARRY. Alright . . . go on.
IAN. What?
HARRY. Go on. *(They look at each other)* Go on . . . it's nineteen sixty five.
IAN. It's nineteen sixty five. . . .
HARRY. It's nineteen sixty five.

HARRY *holds open interior door for* IAN.

IAN. Yeah. *(Goes to door, hesitates.)* It's nineteen sixty five?
HARRY. It's nineteen sixty five.
IAN. Yeah . . . the sleeping-bag.
HARRY. Leave it to me.

IAN *looks at* HARRY *waiting for him to say more.* HARRY *doesn't.* IAN *exits.* HARRY *shuts door behind him. Determinedly and with feverish movements prepares sleeping-bag.*

ACT TWO

Scene 1

Next day. The pub. Morning. Fresh. Brisk. Sunny. ANDREW *is polishing glasses* ALBERT *walks in.*

ANDREW. Good morning Albert.
ALBERT. Did I disgrace myself last night?
ANDREW. I beg your pardon?
ALBERT. Did I order a pasty?
ANDREW. You ate it in the toilet.
ALBERT. Alright?
ANDREW. No complaints.

ANDREW *draws a pint.* ALBERT *pays.* ANDREW *draws himself one.*

ALBERT. It rained last night.

ANDREW. I don't mind.

ALBERT. You don't care whether it rains or shines.

ANDREW. When you've been through what I've been through.

ALBERT. Don't you get lonely out here?

ANDREW. No, I've got the dog. She left the dog . . . I have my job to do.

ALBERT. That dog won't last much longer.

ANDREW. It will last as long as I require it.

ALBERT. What will you do when it dies?

ANDREW. I shall get another dog . . . an old one. It seems silly to wait so long.

ALBERT. Eh?

ANDREW. For a dog. . . .

ALBERT. Wait for a dog. . . .

ANDREW. Wait for a dog to grow old . . . when all you've got to do is get hold of an old dog.

ALBERT. In the first place.

ANDREW. Precisely.

ALBERT. You don't see many old dogs for sale.

ANDREW. No.

ALBERT. You think you could get hold of one?

ANDREW. I've got my eye on one or two.

ALBERT. You're ready.

ANDREW. I don't want to be caught . . . eh . . . with my trousers down again. Now then Albert . . . now then . . . that's enough of that. Be a good fellow.

HARRY *comes in with suitcase and typewriter in case.*

HARRY. Good morning. Pint please.

ANDREW. Are you going somewhere? Good morning . . . pint.

ALBERT. Are you going somewhere?

HARRY. Yes. I am leaving this godforsaken nature preserve forever . . . forever. The sound of grass . . . eh . . . growing . . . is driving me mad. I'd rather live in the middle of Piccadilly Circus.

ANDREW. That'll be Director's bitter?

HARRY. Ordinary.

ALBERT. Going to London?

HARRY. I don't know where I'm going. From . . . is the operative word. I am going from. No doubt I shall land up somewhere . . . where sanity prevails.

ANDREW. When are you coming back?

ALBERT. If you see any old dogs in London. . . .

ANDREW. Alright Albert.

ALBERT. Sorry Andrew.

HARRY. I've said I'm not coming back. This is a farewell drink. Have one . . . three whiskies please.

ANDREW. It's a bit early . . . thank you.

ALBERT. If you see any young bits of crumpet in London. . . .

HARRY. I shall not be looking for that. I am going for space . . . to be hemmed in by strangers. One stranger is an entirely disruptive force . . . the more strangers there are the safer . . . the more lonely. Two strangers meet in a desert . . . it's impossible. Strangers have to be taken in large quantities . . .

eh . . . ha. If you want peace of mind. . . .

ANDREW.   What about that young fellow . . . with the long hair.

HARRY.   What?

ALBERT.   He was a stranger.

ANDREW.   Didn't you put him up?

HARRY.   I don't care. I don't care whether I put him up or not. I have nothing left to care about, thank God, except my work. A great release . . . a tremendous release. I'm on the road.

ANDREW.   When will Ivy catch you up?

HARRY.   Ivy . . . Ivy . . . Ivy . . . a woman. You see a woman . . . need more be said?

ANDREW.   Certainly not . . . it was raining last night and that's good enough for me.

ALBERT.   I wouldn't mind a bit of crumpet.

ANDREW.   Now then Albert.

HARRY.   You speak from ignorance and frustration.

ALBERT.   It's been a long while.

HARRY.   You're lucky . . . you have serenity.

ALBERT.   I don't want that. I got plenty of that to spare . . . for a bit of crumpet.

HARRY.   What about your piano playing?

ALBERT.   Nobody cares about that. I play that piano . . . till opening time . . . after opening time . . . after closing time. I play the piano . . . course I do. I brought it down here . . . to play. And my God I play it. What I'm saying is I could do with a bit of crumpet.

HARRY.   Wish I'd brought a piano down here . . . but I feel tremendous. Great sense of relief . . . walking over the fields . . . wet shoes . . . fine day . . . everything washed. I shall get slightly drunk. I shall catch the one o'clock bus . . . and the two o'clock train. I might not . . . might stay till closing time.

ANDREW.   Be careful about your language.

HARRY.   Cheers. *(Downs whisky in one gulp.)*

OTHERS.   Cheers. *(Drink it more slowly.)*

HARRY.   I put my case outside here at seven o'clock.

ANDREW.   Did you?

HARRY.   Yes I've been walking . . . couldn't sleep. There's hardly anything in that case. Silly to bring it . . . I should have left everything behind.

ALBERT.   Couldn't you sleep? I don't know, you young men with your wives . . . and then you get up and go traipsing round the fields. You could be in a warm bed.

HARRY.   Bed?

ALBERT.   Bed . . . by God . . . bed. I wouldn't mind a bit of bed.

HARRY.   The thought repulses me. Bed? Destroy all beds. If we all slept standing up there wouldn't be half the trouble in this world.

ANDREW.   Here here.

HARRY.   You see Andrew, you know. . . .

ANDREW.   Don't get upset Harry . . . there's long life ahead.

HARRY.   Dahh.

ANDREW.   There's the path. Walk on . . . and on . . . that's the way. Look not to the left . . . nor to the right.

HARRY. God knows what you'll see in the hedgerows . . . their filth . . . their litter. Another whisky. *(ANDREW fetches him another.)*

ALBERT. What happened to that young lad you took home last night?

HARRY. I taught him to play the piano.

ALBERT. Look after him, did you?

HARRY. I feel sick.

ALBERT. He din't take nothing did he? He looked alright . . . smelt a bit.

HARRY. Oh don't talk rubbish.

ALBERT. He din't look the taking sort.

HARRY. And I don't look the giving sort.

ALBERT. You're too generous.

HARRY. Dahh.

ALBERT. Generosity . . . it will get you into trouble. Don't get in the habit of it. There's no end to generosity.

ANDREW. I like a man who'll stand his round.

ALBERT. That's not being generous.

ANDREW. I was saying that I like a man who'll stand his round . . . no more no less.

ALBERT. You haven't seen generosity like I have Andrew . . . been near it. It's frightening. I knew a man once . . . he was generous. He shot himself. He extended, don't you see.

ANDREW. Extended?

ALBERT. Beyond his means. We're not bloody eskimos.

HARRY. Albert is intelligent. God knows why he's carted a piano to the middle of this game reserve . . . to play in a tin hut in the middle of the moors.

ALBERT. Because I don't like it . . . but there's a lot worse.

HARRY. Do you listen to the radio?

ALBERT. Course I do. I like to hear the girls talking. Then I write on a bit of paper.

HARRY. By the piano.

ALBERT. What I think they're wearing. I turn the radio off . . . and concentrate . . . every stitch. Then I turn it on again. The intonation of voice, boy. You can tell what colour knickers they're wearing.

HARRY. You are a very lucky man. You have solved . . . I shall buy a piano, a game reserve, a pair of knickers.

ANDREW. Are you going on the train?

HARRY. I am drinking. I am happy . . . cleansed.

IAN *walks in. Hesitates in door when he sees* HARRY. *Then comes in.*

HARRY. Hello.

IAN. Hi.

HARRY. Have a drink?

IAN. Are you sure?

HARRY. I'm rich . . . have one. I'm a furious writer.

IAN. Furious?

HARRY. My literary capacity. Pint?

IAN. Please.

ANDREW. One pint of ordinary.

HARRY. How are you? How are you?

IAN.   Fine.

HARRY.   Did you have breakfast?

IAN.   Yeah . . . do you mind?

HARRY.   No of course not. What did you have?

IAN.   Eggs . . . bacon . . . you know.

HARRY.   How many eggs?

IAN.   Two I think.

HARRY.   And she. . . .

IAN *(pause).*   Cooked it.

HARRY.   Of course . . . of course . . . of course naturally. She cooked it. This
    is Albert the phantom pianist. He got on a train at Euston with his piano and
    played all the way to Penzance. He was left luggage for a fortnight playing like
    hell . . . blushing no doubt. And then he transported to the moors where a tin
    shed was built round him. He emerged at opening time.

ALBERT.   You were staying with Harry were you, last night?

IAN.   Yeah . . . thank you.

ALBERT.   I saw you go off together. Give you the floor did he?

IAN.   Yeah.

ALBERT.   Well he's generous. It's where to stop is the problem. I wouldn't
    have no one sleeping under my piano . . . 'cos I wouldn't know where to stop.

IAN.   It was very nice. Ivy . . . his wife. . . .

ANDREW.   We know.

IAN.   Cook . . . cooked some breakfast. Harry was out having a walk. We
    waited . . . and then went on and ate.

HARRY.   You can keep eating.

IAN.   I had a bath. I hope you don't mind.

HARRY.   Yes . . . yes . . . it's still the same. It's only tomorrow already . . .
    space of a few hours. Course you had a bath . . . back scrubbed.

IAN.   Eh?

HARRY.   Could you reach it?

IAN.   Harry.

HARRY.   Don't worry. Have a drink.

IAN.   I've got a message for you.

HARRY.   Have a drink. Two whiskies please . . . and I'll have another pint.

ANDREW.   Certainly.

IAN.   She says. . . .

HARRY.   Never mind . . . never mind. Relax.

IAN.   She was upset when you took the case.

HARRY.   You can take the case back. I am naked . . . as a new born. Leave the
    typewriter, I'll need that . . . one day soon. You'll find a few clothes in that
    case.

IAN *indicates sleeping-bag and rucksack on floor.*

IAN.   I'm travelling.

HARRY.   You were last night. I'm travelling. Get on a train . . . oh nonsense.

IAN.   You better go home.

HARRY.   You don't know where to draw the line do you. I know when I'll go
    home. I decide when I leave. I decide when you leave.

IAN.   I left.

HARRY. Would you take a message back?

IAN. Yeah.

HARRY. I thought you were travelling.

IAN. I'll do you a good turn.

HARRY. You want to know how the land lies?

IAN. Well . . . yeah.

HARRY. Do you think you've suddenly become important?

IAN. I'm a human being.

HARRY. Sequences were set in motion . . . a long time ago. And you're a human being . . . right. I don't complain at that.

IAN. I thought you . . . might.

HARRY. I must admit I hadn't noticed. I had other things on my mind. Now you draw my attention . . . my attention . . . to the fact that you're a human being. You've left it a bit late.

IAN. I thought you knew.

HARRY. The rucksack . . . the sleeping-bag . . . it didn't cross my mind.

IAN. I always thought of you as one . . . right from the start.

HARRY. I can't see what difference that's made.

IVY *comes in.*

IVY *(to* HARRY*).* Are you coming home?

HARRY. Go away.

IVY. Are you coming home?

HARRY. Go away. *(*IVY *exits.)*

ANDREW. I think she wants to see you Harry.

HARRY. Ships that pass in the night.

IAN. Why don't you. . . .

HARRY. I'm in charge.

IAN. I know.

HARRY. I know what I'm doing.

IAN. Yeah . . . I know.

HARRY. I wish I didn't.

IAN. Yeah. *(Pause)* What's the message?

HARRY. The message . . . to all mankind. If you want to have an accident . . . drive!

IVY *enters.*

IVY. Are you coming?

HARRY. Go home.

IVY. I want to talk to you.

HARRY. Go home. *(*IVY *exits.)* I shall proceed to pile body on top of body. Do you know what I'm talking about?

IAN. No.

HARRY. I shall continue the search . . . women. But I am determined not to find. I shall sample. I won't investigate. And if a child. . . .

IAN. You got a child?

HARRY. He sleeps late.

IAN. Oh . . . yeah. *(Drinks)* I better be going.

HARRY. What's the matter?

IAN. No . . . it's. . . .

HARRY. What? You're not moral?

IAN. I'm a human being.

HARRY. Damn that. We're all animals . . . or piano players.

IVY *(at door)*. Are you coming?

HARRY. Get out! *(IVY exits.)*

ANDREW. We don't want any quarrelling on the premises Harry. Plenty of room outside.

ALBERT. Don't break my piano.

PHIL *and his* GIRLFRIEND *come in.*

HARRY. A large whisky . . . another pint . . . you? *(To* IAN.*)*

IAN. Ta.

HARRY. And another large whisky . . . and another pint.

IAN. I'm getting sozzled.

HARRY. Enjoy yourself . . . only live once.

IAN. Yeah.

PHIL. What do you want?

GIRL. Cherry brandy.

PHIL. Cherry brandy and a pint please.

ANDREW. Ordinary or director's sir?

PHIL. Director's.

ANDREW. Naturally.

HARRY. Director's . . . and a director's cherry brandy. Excuse me I mean no harm. My friend and I have been described as human beings . . . a mistake anyone could make. Are you down here on your holidays?

PHIL. Yes.

GIRL. Yes.

HARRY. Taking the bracing air? Just married are you?

GIRL. 'Bout a year.

HARRY. And this is your first holiday?

PHIL. Yes.

HARRY. Must be hell. Don't mind me . . . I'm married too and this . . . is a friend of the family. Do you want a friend of the family?

IAN. Are you travelling? Got a motor have you?

PHIL. We're going to London.

HARRY. There you are . . . complete with rucksack . . . all ready. One friend of the family . . . two eggs for breakfast.

IAN. You could drop me off Saint Hilary's Mount.

GIRL. We have got room for one.

HARRY. You could take me.

PHIL. We could take one of you.

IAN. I don't mind.

HARRY. Then it's settled. We'll all stay here and get drunk. When the floods come . . . when we're up to our neck . . . we will grope in the depths . . . the friendly feel beneath the waves. And so goodnight.

ALBERT *(to* IAN*)*. How are you travelling?

IAN. I don't mind.

ALBERT. Be careful . . . people live here.

IAN. I know.

HARRY. It's alright . . . it's alright Albert. I'll look after him.

ALBERT. You want your head seen to.

HARRY. You want to go and tune that piano of yours. If it was so easy we'd all be falling off logs. *(To the couple.)* So return to the city . . . enriched.

IVY *(at door).* Are you coming?

HARRY. Piss off!

IVY. I mean it.

HARRY. Go away. *(IVY exits. IAN goes to follow. HARRY puts hand on his arm.)* Where are you going?

IAN. To see if she had a message for you.

HARRY. We can do without your assistance.

IAN. Sure.

HARRY. And so the young couple . . . who have holidayed . . . do you row?

GIRL. No.

PHIL. What about?

HARRY. My God the sleep of death. Have aother cherry brandy.

GIRL. No thank you.

HARRY. Yes. One cherry brandy and another pint . . . whisky for me and Ian.

IAN. I'm alright.

HARRY. That's another matter altogether.

PHIL. Alright ta.

ANDREW. Same again . . . sort of.

ALBERT. Ta.

HARRY. And so the absurd young couple . . . throw their bodies into the future . . . at some fifty miles an hour . . . confident. Are you CND?

GIRL. What?

HARRY. What are you?

PHIL. What, all that long haired nonsense?

HARRY. The bomb is not long-haired my friend.

PHIL. I believe in minding my own business.

HARRY. Then why did you marry? I bet you've got a safety harness inside your car?

PHIL. Yes.

HARRY. There you are Ian.

IAN. Fine.

HARRY. Look after yourself.

IVY *appears again.*

IVY. I've got the baby out here.

HARRY. He's yours. You'll get the maintenance.

IVY. I've got to look after the baby. *(She exits.)*

HARRY. The smashing of moral systems. A moral system . . . one . . . is . . . with the help of this . . . health maniac here . . . still difficult.

IAN. Count me out.

HARRY. Thank you.

ANDREW. Now then.

HARRY. What?

ANDREW.   Turning into a session. Advance notice . . . good behaviour in the mess.

HARRY.   Of course, Andrew. The line of fire. Do you ever think . . . that somewhere a German is on the Bavarian plains . . . with his iron cross and inn and a few tourists. Now tell me . . . who won?

ANDREW.   We won.

HARRY.   But out of you two?

ALBERT.   About equal.

ANDREW.   I bore no grudge.

HARRY.   The plains of Europe lie waiting . . . pockets of struggle . . . privacy . . . marriage . . . the rights of the individual. Whole countries carved up. the bomb, the long-haired bomb. They'll be so busy arguing they won't hear it arrive.

IAN.   That's good man.

HARRY.   Good Old Ian. Squeeze the lemon . . . you'll have some stories to tell.

IAN.   No.

PHIL.   Well drink up.

GIRL.   Yes.

IAN.   Can I have a lift?

PHIL.   Come on. *(To* HARRY*)* Nice meeting you.

HARRY.   We didn't meet. I'm sorry you didn't notice. And the girl. *(Kisses* GIRL*)* Have you met? *(Indicates her husband)* Take my advice, don't . . . rear your family . . . small size . . . lawn . . . frig . . . all that. There's no need to get initmate with your wife to do that. Just keep going.

PHIL.   Where do we turn left?

ANDREW.   At the bridge . . . sharp left. Thank you for your custom. Goodday, pleasant drive.

GIRL.   Bye bye.

ALBERT.   If you see any old dogs. . . .

ANDREW.   I've got an old dog.

ALBERT.   They might be down next year.

IAN *has picked up his rucksack. Holds hand out to* HARRY.

IAN.   Cheers . . . see you. *(*HARRY *shakes his hand.)*

HARRY.   Long ago . . . and far away . . . the bomb dropped. Desolation . . . deformity . . . nobody noticed . . . nobody noticed. . . .

IAN.   Great, man.

IAN *exits with* PHIL *and the* GIRL. *Sound of car starting up.*

HARRY.   One large whisky. *(*IVY *comes in.)* Have you said goodbye?

IVY.   The baby wants an orange.

HARRY.   The baby wants an orange. Andrew . . . the baby wants an orange.

ANDREW.   One orange for the baby.

Scene 2

Café on harbour front. Sunny. Later same morning. In window sit JENNY *and her sister* RUTH *(two years older).* JENNY *pours tea.*

JENNY. That's the trouble with these birth pills. . . .

RUTH. What dear?

JENNY. You got to remember what day it is.

RUTH. You get a card. You take one off and that's another day gone.

JENNY. Yeah but how can you remember if you took one off?

RUTH. Well if it's gone, dear. . . .

JENNY. That might be the day before . . . you could be taking the pills every five minutes, you don't know. You look at the card, you think your month's past . . . and then you're worried when you don't come on.

RUTH. It's always difficult for you dear. Can't you tell one day from the next?

JENNY. Not when I'm taking them bloody things. Two lumps?

RUTH. Please . . . and another.

JENNY. I prefer the old stretch and repent.

RUTH. That's why you're always getting into trouble isn't it? Stupid moo. Don't like these curtains.

JENNY. You never did like yellow, Ruth.

RUTH. I did . . . not on curtains.

JENNY. You didn't. I can't ever remember you liking yellow.

RUTH. I liked that yellow sweater.

JENNY. Which one?

RUTH. The one you took.

JENNY *(eating cake messily).* Aren't they sticky?

RUTH. What you doing down here this year?

JENNY. Resting.

RUTH. Old Feeler'll give you a job.

JENNY. He's not feeling me this year . . . stick his caff. I'm not an animal.

RUTH. You've got to have money, Jen.

JENNY. I'm not asking you to keep me. Just 'cos you landed old Osborne this year. Old doodle dan the dustbin man.

RUTH. He's alright.

JENNY. He won't throw anything away will he?

RUTH. I make him have a clear out every month.

JENNY. I did not take that yellow sweater.

RUTH. I think you should work down here this year.

JENNY. You don't work.

RUTH. I got Osborne.

JENNY. I could have had Osborne if I'd stayed down last winter.

RUTH. You leave him alone.

JENNY. I wouldn't touch him.

RUTH. Nor would I, dear.

JENNY. He's a nobody person.

RUTH. He's a yesterday man dear. He's quite sweet really.

JENNY. I'd rather work with Old Feeler than live with him.

RUTH.   You're staying with me.

JENNY.   It's not my fault you're living with him.

RUTH.   And don't bring any boys back.

JENNY.   There's plenty of beach, dear.

RUTH.   There's plenty of sand as well.

JENNY.   Errr. . . .

RUTH.   Try the bus stop.

JENNY.   I'm not that hard up. *(IAN appears outside the window. Presses face against window.)* Oh Gawd. . . .

IAN *grins and waves.*

RUTH.   Who's that?

JENNY.   Father Christmas. *(IAN enters.)*

IAN.   Hi. *(Sits with them.)* I apologise . . . Jenny.

JENNY.   What?

IAN.   Yeah. I abandoned you . . . you . . . out phoning trying to fix up a pad for me and you . . . and I walk off. I can't describe it.

JENNY.   I don't care where you walked, I didn't come back to the pub.

IAN.   Jen . . . women. Listen to me. I am sorry for what I did to you.

JENNY.   You didn't do anything. How could you?

IAN.   I'm talking about principles. What's the matter? I am apologising. Can't you take a simple apology? I don't care whether you came back to the pub. I abandoned you.

JENNY.   You didn't.

IAN.   I did.

JENNY.   You could have. It don't make sense. I abandoned you, if anything.

IAN.   What?

JENNY.   I walked out first.

IAN.   Look. *(Holds her lapel.)* I am sorry . . . woman.

JENNY.   Take your hand off my clothes.

IAN *shakes his head. Most of his movements are like a boxer. Picks up cake. Studies it. Eats it.* RUTH *gets up. Gives note to* JENNY.

RUTH.   That's for us two, dear. Don't forget the change.

IAN *(as RUTH walks out).*   Ta. Hey! (She's gone.) Is that your sister?

JENNY.   Yes.

IAN.   Nice bit of goods. I got a job down the amusement arcade.

JENNY.   What are you — one of the amusements?

IAN.   Funny. I got a scheme, Jen. I had a laugh.

JENNY.   What?

IAN.   Yeah . . . ha. Why don't you pretend to be pregnant again?

JENNY.   What?

IAN.   Laugh.

JENNY.   What?

IAN.   I find the blokes. You . . . say you're in the puddin' . . . clean up.

JENNY.   What you think I am — a body?

IAN.   Laugh.

JENNY.   You laugh. Cheek. I didn't know I wasn't pregnant before.

IAN.   You never have to know. Look, they like it . . . burkes. . . .

JENNY. I only go with the men I like.

IAN. There's plenty of them. We'll find some. Don't worry . . . work our way along the coast. Laugh.

JENNY. You laugh. I'm not a whore.

IAN. This isn't . . . eh . . . where? No. Listen. Ahhh . . . forget it.

JENNY. How would you like to pretend you're pregnant?

IAN. Forget it. I got it lined up . . . nice people. Wha . . . what's the matter with you . . . serious?

JENNY. I think you're barmy.

IAN. Yeah.

JENNY. I wish you wouldn't worry me.

IAN. Eh?

JENNY. I think we should both go our own ways now we're down here.

IAN *(getting up)*. Sure . . . sure. Pay for the cake, will you.

IAN *exits.* JENNY *lets him go then pays the bill. Outside the café she sees* RUTH *sitting on the beach. Joins her.*

RUTH. Did you get rid of the monster?

JENNY. He's alright.

RUTH. He's a nobody.

JENNY. Aren't they all? Here, you know what. . . .

RUTH. What dear?

JENNY. I think I'm overdue again.

RUTH. Again? How much?

JENNY. Two weeks.

RUTH. It's nerves. What you worried about?

JENNY. I'm worried about being pregnant.

RUTH. Not him?

JENNY. Yes.

RUTH. Why don't you tell him?

JENNY. Don't know. He won't believe me.

RUTH. What?

JENNY. Anyway what's the point . . . he hasn't got no money to help. Any money I get, he'll spend. Have to be like a barrage balloon before he believed.

RUTH. Osborne went.

JENNY. Oh don't worry about Osborne.

RUTH. He don't believe in it.

JENNY. He's not religious, he's mean.

RUTH. I helped you last summer, Jen.

JENNY. I'll help myself this summer.

Scene 3

Farmhouse kitchen. Late evening. IVY *is reading.* HARRY *at table with typewriter. Takes a shoe and sock off and rubs his feet.*

IVY. Are you picking your feet again?

HARRY. Helps me think.

IVY.   Smells.

HARRY.   I'll wash 'em in a minute. I'm just concentrating.

IVY.   I can't concentrate, I can't read . . . not with that going on. You're either picking your feet or your nose or your ears. Pick, pick, pick. Else you're letting off or something. (HARRY *laughs.*) I don't think it's funny. I have to live with it.

HARRY.   No, I know. Life has lost its romance. I won't do it again.

IVY.   You're scratching your leg now.

HARRY.   Am I?

IVY.   You don't know what you're doing half the time, do you?

HARRY.   No . . . my mind is elsewhere . . . on the profound things of life. You know, darling . . . what is the purpose of marriage? Procreation . . . feet-picking . . . must all fit to a pattern somewhere, eh. . . .

IVY.   Balls.

HARRY.   I feel you're losing respect for me.

IVY.   Course I'll lose respect if you sit around picking your feet all night.

HARRY.   I was thinking about us. It's painful . . . that boy. . . .

IVY.   Forget it.

HARRY.   But why?

IVY.   Does it matter?

HARRY.   Why did you do it?

IVY.   You . . . you ask me that?

HARRY.   You didn't have to.

IVY.   You sent him up.

HARRY.   You could have sent him down again.

IVY.   Oh shutup. It meant nothing . . . forget it.

HARRY.   Nothing? You're sure?

IVY.   I'd rather you picked your feet.

HARRY.   Say you got pregnant. . . .

IVY.   I am not.

HARRY.   Why?

IVY.   Harry . . . of course.

HARRY.   What?

IVY.   I was careful.

HARRY.   Careful? Careful! Don't talk to me about being careful.

IVY.   I'm sorry. I wouldn't have done it if I knew it was going to hurt you so much.

HARRY.   Yes . . . thank you.

IVY.   You're not an angel. You've done it to me for years.

HARRY.   Eh?

IVY.   You don't like a taste of your own medicine, do you?

HARRY.   Is that what it was? I wondered. You did it out of revenge, did you?

IVY.   Oh don't be silly. I'm trying to read . . . forget it.

HARRY.   I can't forget it. I'm going to write about it.

IVY.   Well don't show it to me.

HARRY.   Thank you. Listen . . . put that book down. Why did you do it? What do you mean you were careful? How? What?

IVY.   Do you want me to describe the whole thing?

HARRY.   Yes . . . no. I don't know.

IVY. He came outside.

HARRY. Did he? That was very nice of him.

IVY. What about all the girls you've been with.

HARRY. It's not the same.

IVY. Balls.

HARRY. I am not responsible for the mores of our society.

IVY. What's that?

HARRY. I don't know . . . but. . . .

IVY. Yes . . . some things are alright for men but they're not alright for women, are they? Balls. You're making me angry . . . let me read.

HARRY. I'm angry . . . I'm angry.

IVY. Are you? Are you?

HARRY. You've probably ruined our marriage.

IVY. You brought him home from the pub. I didn't ask you . . . to go out and bring a man home.

HARRY. Why not? Why not?

IVY. Eh?

HARRY. You might as well.

IVY. You'd like that would you?

HARRY. You might as well . . . the way things are going.

IVY. Would you like that?

HARRY. Course I wouldn't — it's got to stop. That's it! That's it!

IVY. Course it is. Don't make a mountain out of a molehill.

IVY *picks up her book.* HARRY *fiddles with his typewriter.*

HARRY. Did you enjoy it?

IVY. Harry!

HARRY. Did you? I've got to know.

IVY. A little bit.

HARRY. A little bit? What do you mean a little bit?

IVY. Alright.

HARRY. Alright? Alright was it?

IVY. Stop jumping down my throat. I shall do as I please.

HARRY. What?

IVY. Yes.

HARRY. What do you mean?

IVY. I've got the same rights as you. I shall very likely not want to go with any-body else for the rest of my life — including you.

HARRY. But if you do?

IVY. It's you . . . you made me like this. You preached your free love at me for years . . . dancing with other women in front of me when I was pregnant . . . mauling them . . . my friends' wives. But you can't take it yourself, can you?

HARRY. I thought you might be a little understanding . . . not just want revenge. You are not seeing that boy again.

IVY. I don't want to see him.

HARRY. He's not coming near you.

IVY. Oh stop being stupid. I don't want him.

HARRY. But if you did, you'd go off again.

IVY. Yes . . . I might not. Might not be worth all the fuss of you carrying on.

Just belt up will you or I might do something.

HARRY. What?

IVY. I don't want men handed to me on a plate by his lordship, thank you.

HARRY. I see . . . you mean. . . .

IVY. I don't mean anything.

HARRY. You mean you would prefer to choose your own lovers.

IVY. How would you like it if I brought stray girls back?

HARRY. Mmmmm. . . .

IVY. Yes you would, wouldn't you. You'd fuck anything.

HARRY. I wouldn't.

IVY. Some of the things you've been with make me sick . . . make me ashamed. Old ladies. . . .

HARRY. Old ladies? What old ladies?

IVY. Anything . . . anything you can get . . . as long as your doodle isn't hanging out all night. You're like an animal. And then you turn round to me. . . .

HARRY. Hang on. . . .

IVY. If I see anybody I like. . . .

HARRY. What?

IVY. Oh shutup.

HARRY. If you see anybody you like you will go with them?

IVY. It's very unlikely.

HARRY. Oh thank you.

IVY. Just stop behaving like the Lord and Master.

HARRY. I am the Lord and Master. I am the Lord and Master. Don't I pay the bills?

IVY. Don't I work in this house . . . and get nothing for it? Except a few rags. I go out . . . I'd be lucky to find a . . . boy . . . the way you dress me.

HARRY. I'll tear up every bloody thing you've got.

IVY *takes dresses from cupboard and throws them at* HARRY.

IVY. Go on tear them up! Tear them up! Tear them up! Thank you! Thank you very much! Tear them! Tear them up go on!

HARRY. No . . . now stop being stupid.

IVY. Shall I do it for you darling? Shall I darling? Shall I darling, shall I?

HARRY. Shutup.

IVY. Eh love . . . shall I? Give it here . . . give to mummy . . . give mummy her rags . . . give mummy her horrible rags!

They struggle with the clothes.

HARRY. Don't tear that dress. I paid money for that! *(*IVY *rips dress.)* You bitch!

IVY. Ahh . . . oh dear . . . look what I've done.

HARRY. Leave them alone.

IVY. Shall I put them on the fire? Shall I put my rags on the fire? Keep daddy warm shall I?

HARRY. They're good dresses — you're not getting any more.

IVY. I can go about naked. You'd like that . . . we'll find some young man. Let me put them on the fire.

HARRY *jumps on her and pulls her to the ground.*

HARRY.   Stop it . . . stop it . . . stop it.

IVY.   That's right, get violent — that's what you were after! Go on hit me! Mark me! Mark me! You've got me in the middle of the moors! No one can hear!

HARRY.   I don't want them to hear.

IVY.   Go on hit me — that's what you want.

HARRY.   I'll smack your bottom.

IVY.   Oh isn't he a big strong boy . . . he'll smack my bottom. He'll smack my bottom, isn't he strong. . . .

HARRY.   Just shutup!

IVY.   Help! Help! Help! Police!

HARRY.   There's no police around.

IVY.   Course there's not! You bastard! You made sure of that! Go on pull my hair harder! Harder! Knock my head on the floor!

HARRY.   I will if you don't shutup.

IVY.   You're doing it.

HARRY.   Am I? Good! Good! **Gooooood!**

IVY.   You're killing me!

HARRY.   Splendid! Splendid!

IVY.   Help! Help!

HARRY.   You'll wake the baby! Shutup!

IVY.   What you going to do — strangle me?!

HARRY.   Yes. Any minute.

Gets his hand round her throat. Stares at her. Pushes her away and gets up, Ivy *moans amongst her dresses on the floor.*

IVY.   Ohhhhhh you bastard . . . you bastard . . . you bastard . . . ohhhh you bastard you bastard . . . ohhhh you bastard. (HARRY *opens door.)* Go on and go and get drunk!

HARRY.   Thank you. *(He exits, slamming door.)*

IVY.   Go on! Get it down your gullet! Drink your rotten money! Pour it down your throat! We've got plenty! I've got my rags! *(Sobs)* Bastard, bastard, bastard. *(Blows her nose loudly on a dress)* Go on you . . .go on . . . go on.

HARRY *comes back and stands in the doorway. She notices him.*

IVY.   Shut the door.

HARRY.   Which side do you want me?

IVY.   Shut the door.

HARRY *comes in and shuts the door. Starts picking up dresses and hanging them back in cupboard.*

HARRY.   I won't get drunk. It would be too easy.

IVY.   Don't make a martyr of yourself.

HARRY.   You've blown your nose all over this one.

IVY.   I'm going to wash it.

HARRY.   We'll have an evening in.

IVY.   It's a miracle.

HARRY.   Don't start. Are you alright?

IVY.   I'm bruised . . . my head . . . my wrist.
HARRY.   Do you want a game of cards?
IVY.   No.
HARRY.   Alright.
IVY.   What?
HARRY.   Crib.
IVY.   Alright. My head hurts across here.
HARRY.   Let's forgive and forget.
IVY.   If only you would.
HARRY.   Once I start trying to forget I start remembering again. I've forgotten forever.

ACT THREE

Scene 1

Mid-season party. Lounge of JANE and BABA's home. Arty without being artistic but quite cosy. All ready for party. Barrel of beer, table laid with bread and cheese. Few birthday cards, balloons. French-windows open onto garden. Warm. Dusk. BABA enters in striped pyjamas.

BABA.   Nobody's coming. Nobody's coming . . . you silly cow. It's not good having a party when somebody else is having a party. They won't come to us . . . it's too far. If they've got a choice they'll go somewhere else.

JANE enters in short, flimsy nighty and wellington boots. They are a middle-aged couple.

JANE.   Do you think the wellington boots go?
BABA.   Eh?
JANE.   Do the wellington boots go?
BABA.   Go where?
JANE.   With the nighty. Is it a good effect? Is it kinky . . . gooky. . . .
BABA.   Gooky . . . standing there looking like an idiot. No one's coming — what's it matter what you look like? What the bloody hell do I care? Wear the . . . *(Growls)* Shhh — wear the bloody things on your head. Why didn't you find out if someone else is having another party?
JANE.   Oh it doesn't matter. If they don't want to come to our party, we won't let them come . . . I don't care. I'm not hard up. It's a lovely party.
BABA.   It can't be a lovely party if we don't have anybody come. It will be horrible, just the two of us.
JANE.   Do you think so?
BABA.   I spent money . . . money on that food . . . that barrel. Money . . . four pounds. Wine, cheese . . . money, money, money.
JANE.   It's your birthday.
BABA.   Eh? So that's it . . . 'cos it's my birthday I have to ruin myself, do I? I see now . . .it is my fault to have a birthday on the day when someone else is having a party. It is my fault that I was born on the twenty-third, is that it? Woman? We could have had the party another night. See! Another night!

Another night!

JANE. Now stop that! Or I'll turn this beer on and just let it run . . . all of it.

BABA. No.

JANE. Baba's a bad boy.

BABA. No.

JANE. Don't you get hysterical with me, you beast.

She turns tap on. BABA *rushes over. Shoves her out of the way and turns tap off.*

BABA. Don't! Don't you! Cow! Bitch! I paid four pounds for that barrel.

JANE. Stick your money!

BABA. Drain my life away! My blood! I sweat and slave. It's my birthday and nobody loves me.

JANE. I don't love you when you're being silly . . . not even a teeny weeny bit . . . so there. And I'll kick you with these wellington boots if you dont shut-up. I will, I will.

BABA. Ahhh . . . look . . . let's calm down. These pre-party nerves. Where did you hide the brandy?

JANE. I've forgotten. *(They search.)*

BABA. You hide it from the guests — not me. It's my birthday. *(Finds bottle.)* Damn them . . . who cares? I don't want a bloody party.

JANE. I'm glad there's another party . . . that means we'll really know who likes us.

BABA. Well no one's come. *(Is swigging brandy. Gives* JANE *bottle.)* Ahhh social living — what it is. They just want to ruin . . . take advantage of my birthday . . . pick a weak spot. I should have had these pyjamas tightened . . . the legs.

JANE. You should have had the flap done up.

BABA. What?

JANE. Stitched.

BABA. What?

JANE. Yes.

BABA. What do you think I am — a pansy. Do you think I'm going to take my trousers down every time I pee — do you?

JANE. It wouldn't hurt you. Nobody wants to see your old man.

BABA. Ruin my confidence . . . go on.

JANE. What? What do you want now? What do you want me to say?

BABA. I like to be attractive to other women. It's my birthday. You like it . . . you know you do.

JANE. Ohhhh . . . now . . . do I? Do I? Oh do I? A little teeny bit.

BABA. Ahhh Jane.

JANE. But I'll bite them. I'll bite their ears off if they look at you. If you twist it's bound to come out.

BABA. The twist is out of fashion.

JANE. That won't stop you. *(Door chimes.)*

BABA. I'll fetch it.

As he exits GALILEO *appears at French-windows, a tall ruin wearing a dirty mac over a night-dress. On head a night cap. He laughs.* JANE *sees him. When* GALILEO *laughs it's more a groan . . . or a nervous whimper.*

JANE.   Hello Galileo . . . hello hello hello.

JANE *runs over to him. Turns to make sure her husband is out of the room and kisses him. A quick, passionate embrace.* JANE *looks over her shoulder, and is about to have another go, when* BABA *returns.*

BABA.   Oh it's you.

GALILEO.   Yesss. I cycled here in my night-dress.

JANE.   I told you someone would come. I told you, I told you, I told you.

BABA.   Yes. *(Mutters)* Ring the bell and then come round the bloody back.

GALILEO.   Shall I take my mack off . . . rrrrrrrrrr . . . my night-dress flapped right up . . . rrrrr . . . this car. There was a lady in front.

JANE.   Oh you naughty boy, you are a naughty boy, you deserve a smack. *(Taps his wrist.* GALILEO *groans with pleasure.)*

GALILEO.   I couldn't . . . I couldn't. . . .

BABA.   It's alright, we've got some here . . . have a glass. *(*BABA *draws glass of beer. Muttering.)* why ring the bell . . . why pay three pounds ten for door chimes. . . . *(Gives glass to* GALILEO.*)*

GALILEO.   Happy birthday Baba. Am I the first?

BABA.   And the last probably. There's another party.

GALILEO.   Oh where?

JANE.   Oh no, we're not letting you go . . . no no no . . . no no no no no . . . not now we've caught you . . . in your little night-gown. Doesn't he look lovely?

GALILEO.   Why are you wearing those wellington boots Jane?

JANE.   Oh I don't know . . . one has to wear something.

GALILEO.   Kinky.

JANE.   Do you think so? I thought rather gooky.

GALILEO.   No definitely kinky. What do you say Baba?

BABA.   Eh?

GALILEO.   Kinky or gooky?

BABA.   What?

GALILEO.   Jane's boots.

BABA.   Bloody stupid. I'm going to get dressed in a minute if no one comes.

JANE.   Oh I'd hit you if it wasn't your birthday.

BABA.   I'd give you one right back in your puddin' muncher.

GALILEO.   Rrrrrr . . . were we supposed to wear them?

BABA *(mutters).*   Labour . . . fixing the bell.

JANE.   What dear?

BABA *(mutters).*   My time.

GALILEO.   Wellington boots.

BABA *(mutters).*   My bloody time.

GALILEO.   Is that food for later?

JANE.   Oh he can have some now, can't he Baba?

BABA.   He can dance on the bloody table for all I care.

GALILEO.   Ta. *(Goes to table and eats.)*

BABA.   Wolf it down . . . dig in, dig in.

JANE.   The brie is lovely . . . lovely, lovely.

BABA.   Have the brie, have the cheddar, it's all been paid for.

GALILEO.   I'm peckish.

BABA. Might as well eat it . . . only have to throw it away.

JANE. Have a lovely pickled onion . . . have two . . . have three.

BABA. Why did you ring the bloody bell?

GALILEO *(mouth full)*. What?

BABA. If you're coming round the back. . . . *(GALILEO stares at him.)* Doesn't matter. *(GALILEO starts chewing again.)*

JANE. Course it doesn't. Who cares about a bell? Who cares about a silly bell?

BABA. I bought that bell for three pound ten. You were on about it for ages!

JANE. Well why don't you go out and ring it if you're so fond of it?

BABA. Bloody birthday. Ring the bell, ring the bell, stand on the doorstep ringing the bell at night, make your own fun out here. I am thirty nine. Where have I got in life? What have I got? You. That's all I've got to show for 39 years. You . . . and a thousand bloody chickens out there.

JANE. Don't start blaming me for starting a stupid chicken farm.

BABA. Well I'm not going to blame the chickens am I?

JANE. That's my mother's money.

BABA. Look you can pack those bloody chickens off to her any time you like . . . all I'm saying is I'm thirty nine . . . today . . . and if I can't say that on my birthday. Ohh never mind.

GALILEO. Where's this other party?

BABA. Finished your food have you? You got a barrel of beer to drink yet. *(Door chimes.)*

JANE. Ohh hurrah! Somebody loves us! Somebody loves us! *(Rushes out.)*

BABA. Probably God. Go easy on that cheese Galileo, we've got guests coming.

GALILEO. I'm a guest.

BABA. Do you wear that in bed that, night-dress?

GALILEO. It's a night-gown. I've only got a sleeping bag.

BABA. How can you get in a sleeping bag with that on?

Enter OSBORNE, JENNY and RUTH. OSBORNE is wearing striped pyjamas and a smoking-cap. RUTH wears pyjamas and JENNY a full length nightdress.

OSBORNE. Are we the first?

GALILEO. No I am.

JENNY/RUTH. Hello Gal.

GALILEO. Hello.

JENNY. Oh gawd, don't he look frightful.

RUTH. Where'd you get that from dear, your mother?

JENNY. Probably got his mum in there.

OSBORNE. Happy birthday Baba. *(Gives him bottle of wine.)* Oh I see you've got some birthday cards.

BABA. Yes they're old ones I got out from last year. Have some brandy Osborne?

GALILEO. Brandy?

JANE enters. Now wearing very high-heeled shoes.

JANE *(to RUTH)*. Oh pyjamas — why didn't I think of pyjamas? They're more gooky, aren't they — more promise. Oh no no promises no promises no promises.

RUTH.   Have you got a lot of people coming?

JANE.   Oh yes, you mustn't rush away. Put the music on Ba.

BABA.   Hang on . . . wine?

JANE.   Yes wine . . . wine for the ladies . . . that's how you tell the difference. Ladies drink wine, men drink beer.

OSBORNE.   Hope we get the glasses mixed. *(Laughs)* are those really old cards Baba?

BABA.   No. . . .

GALILEO.   Ahh. What are you doing these days Galileo?

GALILEO.   What?

OSBORNE.   What are you doing these days?

GALILEO.   Huh.

JENNY.   Who's coming Jane?

JANE.   Oh everybody . . . everbody who's really somebody.

RUTH.   It's a long way to get out here.

JANE.   Baba could pay something towards the petrol.

RUTH.   Took ages.

JANE.   I'm sorry . . . am I sorry? No I don't think I'm really sorry . . . not really . . . because I think it's worth it. If I didn't think that I'd have had no right to hold a party, would I? No I wouldn't . . . but I have . . . and we're having one . . . whoopee. *(To JENNY)* Oh a long cotton night-dress that's what we should have worn. I feel so exposed.

RUTH.   You are exposed, dear.

JANE.   Do you think I'm overexposed? Do you? Do you really?

RUTH.   You don't leave much to the imagination, dear.

JANE.   That's better, isn't it? You can't trust their imaginations . . . not these days . . . they're so silly. You have to tell them every little bit. Oh no . . . I'm so glad you've come.

RUTH.   We can't stay very long.

JANE.   I'm sure you can.

BABA *puts on music.* IAN *comes through french-windows. Dress usual. Helps himself to drink.*

BABA.   Hello Ian.

IAN.   Hi. *(Goes over to girls.)*

OSBORNE *(pinholes* BABA*).*   How are you doing?

BABA.   Going to make a lot of money next year, Osborne.

OSBORNE.   I mean you . . . you. . . .

BABA.   I keep fit.

OSBORNE.   I mean you the inner you.

BABA.   Still left wing.

OSBORNE.   Deeper . . . deeper.

BABA.   Steel?

OSBORNE.   No.

BABA.   Bread. *(*OSBORNE *looks at him.)* I break bread. I eat. *(Breaks bread and eats.)*

OSBORNE.   That's better. I remember when you cried all over my car . . . all over my bonnet, do you remember? May I have some of the bread that you have just broken?

BABA.   Sure.

OSBORNE *(eats bread solemnly. Confidentially to* BABA*)*.   Fuck 'em . . . fuck 'em. . . . *(*BABA *nods. Door chimes.)*

JANE.   Oh lovely, lovely more more poeple . . . people, people, people. *(She exits.)*

BABA.   Probably God. *(No one notices remark.)* I said: probably God.

Enter ANDREW *and* ALBERT. ANDREW *in night-shirt, but with sam brown officer's belt.* ALBERT *in pyjamas. They find* BABA.

ANDREW.   Off limits.

BABA.   What?

ANDREW.   Out of bounds. Officers only.

ALBERT.   That's alright then.

ANDREW.   Other ranks down the road.

BABA.   Been drinking this afternoon, have you?

ANDREW.   Don't mix.

BABA.   Drinks?

ANDREW.   No. Officers and men.

ALBERT.   Don't talk shop.

ANDREW.   Haircut Albert.

ALBERT.   Shit, shave and shampoo.

ANDREW.   That's right. Gone she was. In one night. My life changed. Landscape altered. Geography incoherent. Map references indecipherable.

ALBERT.   Don't dwell on it. Dance!

ANDREW.   Thank you. *(They dance.)*

OSBORNE.   Don't wash God out.

BABA.   No.

OSBORNE.   Privately one to another He may survive.

BABA.   In what bloody form . . . that's a universe out there Osborne.

OSBORNE.   I've seen it.

BABA.   Where is God . . . where is God? Does He pay my purchase tax?

OSBORNE.   Take the long term view.

BABA.   I want to export . . . me . . . me. They tell you to export . . . they go on and on — export, export. But will they let me export — no!

OSBORNE.   God's not stopping you exporting. Don't blame the old fellow for that.

BABA.   We see things differently, Osborne. If God is in charge of everything he must be in charge of exports! And they won't let me export! These men of God!

OSBORNE.   Baba.

BABA.   No. No.

OSBORNE.   Baba.

BABA.   I'm sorry.

OSBORNE.   We have broken bread together.

BABA.   I didn't notice. Mix . . . mix.

JANE *comes back. Now in furry slippers and wearing a sleeping-bonnet, if there's any such thing. If there's not, she would have invented it.*

JANE *(to* BABA*).*   It's Ivy and Harry.

BABA.   Good. Maybe I can have some conversation now.

JANE.   Isn't it nice of them?

BABA.   What?

JANE.   To come.

BABA.   What do you mean?

JANE.   No, why should it be nice? They don't have to come. They've come . . . good . . . we don't care that much, do we Ba? We like them . . . take it or leave it. They can all go . . . any minute. We could throw them all out. That Ruth, she wants you to pay her petrol.

BABA.   What are you talking about, woman?

JANE.   I don't know. Should I know? Do you think that's necessary? *(To* OSBORNE*)* Perhaps it's better if we don't know what we're talking about . . . perhaps we'll communicate . . . communicate.

BABA.   Shut up. *(Walks off.)*

OSBORNE *(to* JANE*).*   He's got quite a religious streak.

JANE.   Has he? How gooky . . . or is it kinky . . . I don't know. You tell me Osborne. It's so hard to keep up these days.

HARRY *enters. Jeans and sweater.*

BABA.   Why aren't you wearing pyjamas?

HARRY.   Don't you start. He's here is he?

BABA.   Who?

HARRY.   Yes.

IAN *(from across room).*   Hi.

HARRY.   Hi. *(*IVY *enters in pretty night-dress.)*

HARRY.   Got any brandy? Here's some. Happy birthday. *(Gives* BABA *bottle of brandy.)*

BABA.   Hello Ivy. Oh yes . . . bedtime.

IVY.   Hello Baba, happy birthday. Did you get the card?

BABA.   Card? Card? *(*HARRY *gives him envelope with card.)*

HARRY *(to* IVY*).*   I would have posted it . . . I . . . ohh I'm trying to write a masterpiece, I'm supposed to post letters.

IVY.   Why say you'd do it?

HARRY.   I was trying to help.

BABA *(putting card out).*   Ah, somebody loves me. Bless you. When she says to me that everybody hates me I'll show her the card.

HARRY.   Even sex maniacs get birthday cards.

BABA.   Do they? Filthy swines.

IVY *(aside to* HARRY*).*   Do I look nice?

HARRY.   Great.

IVY.   Are you sure?

HARRY.   Beautiful. Toddle along then.

IVY *looks at* HARRY. *Then walks over to talk to* IAN. HARRY *drinks with* BABA.

RUTH *(with* JENNY*)*.   You should tell him, dear. It makes me sick.

JENNY.   You could get the money off Osborne.

RUTH.   No he won't wear it. He's got right into religion this winter . . . meaner and meaner. You cook an egg — he's down on you let alone an abortion. You should have worked while you had time.

JENNY.   Work's for pigs. I got time.

RUTH.   You haven't got time to get the money working. Ask Ian, ask him. It's his responsibility.

JENNY.   He wouldn't talk to me again. He hasn't got no money.

RUTH.   He could get it.

JENNY.   He'd spend it. He spent the last lot. I got that.

RUTH.   You wasn't pregnant then.

JENNY.   Makes no difference to him. If I looked like a barrage balloon he'd say it was wind.

RUTH.   You don't still like him do you?

JENNY.   Course I don't. I'm not going to let him drop me. He can't go round saying that. I got to live in this town.

RUTH.   He may know someone.

JENNY.   Belt up, I'm alright. *(*IVY *and* IAN *dance.)* Who's he dancing with?

RUTH.   Ivy. She'll talk to you when the wind's in the right direction. He's alright . . . but barmy . . . alright when he's sober.

JENNY.   Who?

RUTH.   Harry.

OSBORNE *and* GALILEO *collide for a moment.*

GALILEO.   I've been thinking about religion.

OSBORNE.   Wouldn't suit you.

GALILEO.   It . . . it brings all sorts of people together.

OSBORNE.   Quite. Excuse me. *(*JANE *bounds up.)*

JANE.   Will you dance with me? *(*GALILEO *grunts.)* I meant Osborne . . . I'm saving you up for later. You're going to be my later . . . my little later . . . are you. I hope so. *(She dances off with* OSBORNE.*)* I do like your pyjamas.

OSBORNE.   They're my every day ones.

JANE.   Oh, how nice. I'm glad you didn't put on anything special . . . just throw on an old pair of pyjamas and come straight over. *(*BABA *and* HARRY *drink.)*

BABA.   Why does it go on from day to day? Day after day . . . yatter yatter yatter yatter. There's no sex left. I daren't leave the baby with her — she might take it out on the baby. I tremble every time she takes the baby for a walk. What's she doing I don't know. Walking down the middle of the road zigzagging. I don't know. I don't know. Headaches, stomach aches, neurosis, a walking knock-shop . . . only time she's well is when we're having parties. What am I going to do — have parties all the time? Tell me . . . tell me.

HARRY.   Yeah . . . well it gives you an interest in life.

BABA.   I lie in bed. I lie there. When she swallows I have to clench my fist. When she yawns . . . oh . . . I know she's taking it out on me. When she sighs . . . I just lie there. Sigh . . . sigh . . . it's all my fault. I'm keeping a damn poultry farm so that she can flap around all day.

HARRY.   Give it up.

BABA.   Throw up my business . . . let her win?

HARRY.   Take the child. Take the chickens. All she'll find's a few feathers when she wakes up in the morning.

BABA.   Ahh man, have some more brandy. I can talk to you. Tell me your problems.

HARRY.I'm not sure what they are any longer. We'll see what happens. I just know that somewhere I feel angry.

BABA.   Great . . . great. *(Slaps* HARRY *on back.)* You and I go through the same problems.

HARRY.   Yeah. Mmm. Keep drinking, partner.

OSBORNE *and* JANE *stop dancing.* GALILEO *sidles round.*

JANE.   Oh you do damn well. You hold yourself a little stiffly . . . you're shy . . . a teeny bit. I won't eat you. Don't be frightened of my husband he likes me dancing . . . so that he can get on with his talking . . . while his silly wife dances with lovely men.

GALILEO.   I think intellectual conversation has had its day.

OSBORNE.   Yes. Excuse me.

OSBORNE *joins* JENNY *and* RUTH. IVY *and* IAN *go out into the garden. Not hand in hand.*

BABA *(sees them).*   Here. . . .

HARRY.   They're friends.

JENNY *(comes up to* HARRY*).*   Do you dance?

HARRY *(to* BABA*).*   You will excuse me, won't you?

BABA.   Don't keep him long.

JENNY.   Alright darling.

BABA.   I've got him marked down on my card.

JENNY.   Are you taking the pill as well? *(as* JENNY *and* HARRY *dance)* You're not saying much tonight.

HARRY.   No.

JENNY.   That's an improvement. You're a writer aren't you?

HARRY.   Yes.

JENNY.   I like writers.

HARRY.   Do you? What authors do you prefer, then?

JENNY.   Young ones.

JENNY *(calls over to* BABA*).*   We were just talking about wee wee, darling.

BABA.   Yes.

GALILEO.   Arrr . . . is there an urge for the female to wet upon the male?

JENNY.   Ohh lovely . . . oohh yes, oh golly. Lovely job.

BABA.   Crap.

GALILEO.   Crap?

JANE.   Oh come on darling, don't be a spoil sport. Wouldn't you love me to winkle over you just a little bit?

BABA.   Can't you talk about politics or something?

JANE.   Oh I know . . . till you get another girl. Then you don't talk politics, do you . . . what? Oh no? Bed talk? But you always blame me.

BABA.   Look if you want to wet over Galileo take him upstiars and wet on him. You can piss off. Bloody birthday.

JENNY *and* HARRY *go and get a drink.*

JENNY.   Don't you mind your wife going in the garden with other men?
HARRY.   There's only fresh air out there, isn't there?
JENNY.   Think what they might be doing.
HARRY.   Shut up.
JENNY.   You're sweet. I know that Ian. Don't trust him.
HARRY.   I hope not.
JENNY.   I came down with him.
HARRY.   You his girl friend?
JENNY.   Have been.
HARRY.   What's he like?
JENNY.   What?

HARRY *takes* JENNY'S *sleeve and takes her out of the room. Grabs bottle of wine on way.* OSBORNE, RUTH *and* BABA *together.*

OSBORNE.   The basis of life is a circle.
RUTH.   I'll say . . . with you it is.
OSBORNE.   It is with everyone, Ruth. Because I concentrate on boredom don't misunderstand me. I make an art of the unavoidable.
RUTH *(yawns)*.   You're very good at it Osborne.
OSBORNE.   Tell me Ruth . . . tell Baba . . . has there been one moment in your seven months and three weeks association when you have not been utterly bored?
RUTH.   No dear. *(Yawns again.)*
OSBORNE.   There!
BABA *(takes* RUTH'S *hand)*.   Come on.
RUTH.   Can you manage to be boring by yourself for a little while darling?
OSBORNE.   Go ahead. *(*BABA *and* RUTH *dance.)*
BABA.   Doesn't he give you the hebejebes?
RUTH.   I didn't know you cared, love.
BABA.   Oh yes . . . yes yes yes.
RUTH.   Don't get carried away.

IVY *comes back in.* IAN *follows.*

IAN.   What's the matter?
IVY.   I don't like to be used, that's all.
IAN.   Sure.
IVY.   I've got a mind of my own.
IAN.   That's it. Ivy . . . listen . . . you got to do what you want to do. Every-one . . . pushing you around . . . am I right?
IVY.   Eh?
IAN.   Don't let him.
IVY.   Let's go and talk to someone else.
IAN.   Ivy.
IVY.   Come on.
IAN.   Drag . . . woman. *(Holds her arm and stops her moving.)* Ivy . . . I just

want to talk to you . . . outside.

IVY. No.

IAN. OK, OK. It's personal . . . straight up . . . you want everyone to hear? *(IVY allows herself to be led outside again.)*

JANE *(to* BABA*).* Are you angry with your wife?

BABA. It doesn't matter.

JANE. I know. It's a very important birthday.

BABA. It's just that . . . Why does nothing ever happen?

JANE. It will, oh it will. I'll tell you a little secret. Ivy and Ian are in the garden.

BABA. And Harry and Jen are locked in the bathroom.

JANE. Oh what a lovely party. All those night-clothes. She's got a lovely nightie.

BABA. Who?

JANE. That girl Jen . . . and Ivy, she looks sweet. She looks nice. All in their nice cuddly nighties — what a good idea.

BABA. The men . . . the men should wear . . . clothes . . . and the women . . . nighties.

JANE. Yes.

BABA. But I am in pyjamas.

JANE. You look lovely.

BABA. Who will talk to me?

JANE. I will dear.

BABA. It's my birthday. I feel like a nit. The men should be in jeans.

JANE. Oh no.

BABA. You said yes.

JANE. Eh?

BABA. A second ago . . . can't you remember what you say? This was your idea, wasnt it . . . pyjamas?

JANE. You haven't had enough to drink.

BABA. Listen . . . you are about the only woman at this damn party who is not being laid. You're my wife.

JANE. I could be laid. Of course I could be laid. I don't care to try much. Galileo would do it like a shot.

BABA. That's worse. My self respect.

JANE. Why don't you dance with me? I'm your wife. I'm your wife. I'm your wife.

BABA. Alright, alright.

JANE. Don't you want to dance with me?

BABA. Of course I do. Come on, let's get it over with. *(JANE and* BABA *dance.)*

RUTH *(with* OSBORNE*).* Why are you so mean?

OSBORNE. Boredom is not enough.

RUTH. I think I've had a bad effect on you.

OSBORNE. Good . . . deeper. By going deep into boredom and meanness . . .

RUTH. You won't find Christ that way. Soon as I get another room I'm moving. I was going to ask you something . . .

OSBORNE. Money?

RUTH.   Forty pounds. *(GALILEO drifts over.)*

GALILEO.   Osborne, did I hear you had a spare room?

OSBORNE.   No.

GALILEO.   I can't paint in my tent. I can't get the easel up and there's not room.

RUTH.   Paint the tent dear — that's made of canvas.

GALILEO.   Heerrrhh yes . . . sss. Like Michelangelo painting the roof of the Sistine Chapel.

RUTH.   Yes well I should see how it turns out. Get some drink dear, will you. Run along there's a good chap.

GALILEO.   Alright. *(GALILEO moves off.)*

RUTH.   Stick your forty pounds. I'm going back to London.

OSBORNE.   You think that . . . you say . . . tell me . . . I should pay for . . . for a sin?

RUTH.   What's eating you? You weren't like this.

OSBORNE.   I don't want to touch your body.

RUTH.   Oh rubbish.

OSBORNE.   I don't, I don't. But other fingers . . . irresponsible . . . with no sense of the universe . . .

RUTH.   I am not up the stick.

OSBORNE.   Oh I see now. I am the collecting house. Let them . . . with their trousers. They can't even dress . . . what . . . why don't they dress for the party in pyjamas? I don't mind their long hair, that's their affair, but they were invited here. This is a pyjama party.

RUTH.   The Lord giveth and the Lord taketh away.

OSBORNE.   You mock me, Ruth. *(GALILEO comes back.)* Ruth . . . the sands are shifting. One person . . . is trying to stand for something.

RUTH.   Utter boredom.

OSBORNE.   I'm sick.

RUTH.   I'm sick . . . sick to death of you, you mean swine.

OSBORNE.   Body.

RUTH.   I've got a body.

OSBORNE.   The arrangement was . . .

RUTH.   You think I'll model for you. You think I'll take my clothes off . . . for you to poke around.

GALILEO.   I'd like to share a model . . . Osborne.

OSBORNE.   You promised three hours a day . . . modelling.

RUTH.   You learn to draw first.

OSBORNE.   Ruth . . . anger I will not. Boredom and meanness I will concentrate on.

RUTH.   There's someone in trouble and you won't help.

GALILEO.   If there were . . . err . . . six of us . . .

OSBORNE.   What?

GALILEO.   That's a shilling each. In the summer there's no electricity.

RUTH.   What are you droning about, Gal?

GALILEO.   I thought it would help.

RUTH.   What?

GALILEO.   If she modelled for six shillings an hour.

RUTH.   Who?

GALILEO. I don't mind.
RUTH. Go and have some more cheese.

GALILEO *goes off. He is grabbed by* JANE.

JANE. Your turn . . . your little turn . . . come along.
GALILEO. Jane . . .
JANE. I know . . . I know, I know. Come on. You're so tall I don't know
  how you fit in that tent.
GALILEO *(as they dance)*. I have to crouch.
JANE. Oh I'd love to crouch with you.
RUTH *(still arguing with* OSBORNE). Your bloody religion. You won't
  help, will you . . . twenty?
OSBORNE. Three hours a day.
RUTH. I'm not taking my clothes off for you. I'm finding another room.
  I'm going to London. I don't know what I'm doing. I wish I had a job . . .
  some independence.
OSBORNE. I will pay five pounds . . . Ruth . . . for one sitting.
RUTH. You mean it?
OSBORNE. Yes.
RUTH. And you'll give up being boring?
OSBORNE. Yes. You'll break me one day.
RUTH. Not at five pounds a time I won't . . . mean old bugger. (HARRY
  returns.)
GALILEO *(dancing)*. Is the toilet free now, Harry?
HARRY. How the hell should I know? Go and have a look.
JANE *(dancing)*. Oh dear what can the matter be . . . who have we found
  locked in the lavatory . . . (GALILEO *whimpers delight.*)
BABA. Mate! Come . . . save me from insanity. Have some brandy!
HARRY. Ta.
BABA. Alright?
HARRY. Eh?
BABA. Never mind.
HARRY. Fine. Where's Ivy?

IVY *comes through window.* IAN *trails after her.*

BABA. Just in time . . .
HARRY. Who me or her? *(*JENNY *comes in.)*
GALILEO. Is the toilet free now, Jen?
JENNY. How the hell should I know? Go and have a look.
JANE *(dancing)*. Oh dear. Ohh dear.
GALILEO. Oh dear what can the matter be . . .
JANE. You've got a little bogey on your nose. I'd love to pick it off.
GALILEO. Eeeeehh . . . *(Dance finishes.* GALILEO *makes for* IAN.)
  Hello Ian.
IAN. Hi.
GALILEO. Any nice flowers in the garden . . . hurrr.
IAN. Get knotted.

GALILEO. Is Jen still your girl friend, Ian?
IAN. Sure . . . man. Leave it.
GALILEO. She was a long time in the toilet.
IAN. So? Listen . . . don't tell me.
GALILEO. So was Harry.

IVY *joins* HARRY *and* BABA.

IVY. Can I have a drink?
BABA. Drop of the hard stuff.

IAN *gets* JENNY *to one side.*

IAN. Listen . . . listen . . . Jen. Great. I mean it. No regrets . . .
JENNY. What?
IAN. Yeah . . . you had to go through with it.
JENNY. What?
IAN. Shut your eyes . . . enjoy it. I don't care. Two months . . . less . . . we
    claim. Bingo.
JENNY. What are you talking about?
IAN. Now Jen. Me . . . *(Taps head.)* . . . Master. mastermind. Yeah listen
    . . . don't get funny . . . I took her old lady . . . his . . . *(Flicks fingers.)* Look
    me out in the garden . . . with her. I leave the field clear for you.
JENNY. Ta.
IAN. You don't mean you didn't . . .
JENNY. Mind your own business.
IAN. Look . . . when we get out of here . . . together . . . together.
JENNY. We're finished.
IAN. Sure. We got a partnership, Jen.
JENNY. Get your hands off me.
IAN. I set it up. You want all the lousy money. Whore . . . whore. I think . . .
    me . . . you collect . . . I think. All you got to do . . . what . . . lean over . . .
    lean over. You get it both ways.
JENNY. You're horrible.
IAN. Hell . . . I . . . look after you.
JENNY. Look after me? You?
IAN. Sure . . . sure, sure.
JENNY. You look after me — that'll be the day.
IAN. Jen.
JENNY. I need looking after. Bastard.
IAN. Come outside.
JENNY. With you, you bastard? You've had it enough, a'nt you to get me
    in trouble?
IAN. What? Come on.
JENNY. Leave me alone. You make me shudder.
IAN. Neurotic. You need me. Talk . . . talk it out . . . Jen.
JENNY. Talk it out, you bastard? How do I talk out I'm in the puddin'?
IAN. Great. Great Jen . . . you . . . no . . . yes . . . you convinced me. That's
    great . . . a team . . . a team.
JENNY. Goodbye.

IAN.   Save it for Harry . . . gear. Come outside, Jen.
JENNY.   No. I hate you. We're finished.
IAN.   Jen . . . ahh . . .

He pulls her. She pulls back. He won't let go. She gives him an almighty slap across the face. Walks off to RUTH. HARRY *and* IVY *are dancing.*

HARRY (*hears slap*).   Ouch. (IVY *cuddles up to him.*) You're affectionate.
IVY.   Let them quarrel. Let the rest of the silly old world argue.
HARRY.   You?
IVY.   I didn't . . . course I didn't. It's you, you fool.

She kisses him as they dance. OSBORNE, RUTH *and* JENNY *are together.*

JENNY.   I want to go home.
RUTH.   Get us a drink Osborne.
OSBORNE.   Please. Please. Please. *(Goes off to get drinks.)*
RUTH.   I can get you some money. I got to strip off before the monster.
JENNY.   Don't do that for me. Oh Ruth.
RUTH.   It won't hurt me. Looks can't kill.
OSBORNE (*returns with the drinks*).   Two pounds.
RUTH.   What?
OSBORNE.   For the first session . . . Breaking the ice . . . say three pounds.
   And then the nominal six shillings an hour. You see it's not fair on the rest
   of the profession to price them out of the market.
JENNY.   She ain't stripping off for you for any three pounds. We can look
   after ourselves. Now drive us home you dirty old man.
OSBORNE.   I am honest.
RUTH.   Bugger.
OSBORNE.   An honest bugger if you like.
RUTH.   You promised.
OSBORNE.   Nothing born out of desire is worth the ashes.
JENNY.   You . . . you, you know what you are. A great lump of it, you are.
   Just 'cos you got you and your precious rooms. Stick 'em. We're not
   animals. Everywhere you turn there's buggers like you . . . poking and
   prying . . . sniffing. What . . . I caught you.
OSBORNE.   Eh?
JENNY.   I come in the room — you were sniffing my knickers, weren't you
   eh? Last night.
OSBORNE.   I gave you that room free.
JENNY.   Go on — sniff, sniff.
RUTH.   You dirty old thing. He shouldn't sniff your knickers.
JENNY.   You're living with him — he should sniff yours if anybody's.
OSBORNE.   Nonsense.
RUTH.   Leave the dirty laundry. Leave it to Osborne. He'll sort it out. And
   we can't even boil an egg.
OSBORNE.   Your soiled garments are everywhere.
JENNY.   Oh dear.
RUTH.   Oh dear . . .
BABA (*joining them*).   Did I hear someone say knickers?

JENNY.   Sniff 'em.

BABA.   Lovely. Where . . . where?

JENNY.   He does.

HARRY.   He's religious isn't he? Probably a religious gesture.

RUTH.   An indecent gesture.

HARRY.   It's better than paying rent, isn't it?

RUTH.   Well . . . of course it is.

JANE (*coming up*).   What am I missing . . . what am I missing?

BABA.   Knickers darling — sniffing of.

JANE.   Oh what a lovely party. Talk some more, talk some more. Talk about knicker elastic — I like that, don't you? Oh I'm going to go and put my boots on. But I don't want to miss anything, so I'll stay. And I want to do a wee-wee. I'm torn! I'm torn!

BABA.   Torn knickers!

JANE.   Let's play guessing games — what colour I'm wearing. (*Cries and guessing. IAN gets IVY to one side.*)

IAN.   Ivy. I am honest to you.

IVY.   Yes, I think so. It doesn't matter.

IAN.   Ivy, I'm not a homebreaker.

IVY.   No.

IAN.   I . . . listen . . . understand. But when that little tramp . . . yes.

IVY.   What?

IAN.   Goes . . . yeah . . . while . . . you and I . . . our backs turned . . . pure. What are we doing? Talking . . . talk . . . chat.

IVY.   What are you telling me?

IAN.   I . . . it doesn't matter. Have they noticed? I am human. Harry . . . a regular feller. Why? What have I done? OK . . . the toilet is locked — anyone could have found them. But we suffer . . . you and me.

IVY.   Thank you.

The music they are dancing to suddenly stops.

ANDREW.   It is finished.

ALBERT.   What?

ANDREW.   This bit.

ALBERT.   Alright.

ANDREW.   Curious precognitiounce.

ALBERT.   Amazing foresight.

ANDREW.   Flavour of the month . . .

ANDREW *collapses. ALBERT catches him as he falls and drags him out. IVY beckons HARRY aside.*

IVY.   I know.

HARRY.   What? Christ . . . look that . . .

IVY.   How could you? I gave us another chance.

HARRY.   How the hell did I know?

IVY.   You.

HARRY.   Ivy, I was stuck. Just thinking . . . outside . . . you and him.

IVY.   I did nothing. I wouldn't let him touch me. He tried hard enough.

HARRY.   I didn't know. I couldn't bear the thought of it.

IVY.   Well why didn't you come outside . . . instead of locking yourself in
the toilet with some dirty slut. You, you live in toilets don't you? Well stay
there. Go in and don't come out! Lock yourself in with who you like, 'cos
it won't be me! *(IVY runs out. HARRY finds BABA.)*

HARRY.   Thanks Baba. Lovely party.

BABA.   Had enough?

HARRY.   Ta.

BABA.   Trouble?

HARRY.   You're joking. 'Night.

As HARRY *leaves, the door bell chimes continuously, just heard over noise
of knicker game.*

JANE *(running out).*   Coming, coming, coming, I say brown for Ruth's
knickers. Keep that for me, Baba. Nigger brown. Ohh *(She soon runs
back in.)* It's them!

BABA.   Who?

JANE.   Everyone. The other nasty party run out of drink and I'm not sorry.
I'm not, I'm not, I'm not. That will teach them to show more respect for
our nighties!

BABA.   What a bloody birthday.

Scene 2

The Pub.
A month later.
ANDREW *and* ALBERT *at bar.*

ANDREW.   And then . . . and then I picked him up. I shook him and I
threw him.

ALBERT.   Threw him?

ANDREW.   Threw him.

ALBERT.   At her?

ANDREW.   Ahh.

ALBERT.   And then you threw the dog at her?

ANDREW.   Aye.

ALBERT.   What was her reaction?

ANDREW.   She barked.

ALBERT.   What — your wife?

ANDREW.   Aye.

ALBERT.   How was the dog?

ANDREW.   Shocked. Absolutely stunned. Off his food for weeks.

ALBERT.   Did you have a licence for him?

ANDREW.   What's that got to do with it?

ALBERT.   Just checking.

ANDREW.   Don't check up on me.

ALBERT.   Then what did she do?

ANDREW.   Drink up.

ALBERT.   Aye.

ANDREW. Out.

ALBERT. Me.

ANDREW. Come on.

ALBERT. Am I barred?

ANDREW. It looks very much like it.

ALBERT. Damn it, damn it.

ANDREW. You'll keep a civil tongue in your head till you step outside that door.

ALBERT. You need my trade in the wintertime, Andrew. Reconsider your position. I can break you. I can cycle into Penzance.

ANDREW. You haven't got a bicycle, Albert.

ALBERT. I could borrow yours . . . friend in need.

HARRY *comes in with* JENNY *She sits down.*

ANDREW. Good evening all.

HARRY. Evening. Pint and a brandy please. You're busy tonight.

ANDREW. Season's nearly finished.

JENNY. I'm cold. *(*HARRY *sits with* JENNY.*)* Well?

HARRY. Well what?

JENNY. What you got to tell me?

HARRY. How did you know?

JENNY. I'm not daft. When's she coming back?

HARRY. Well . . . I was going to tell you what she said. The weekend.

JENNY. Going to give you another chance, is she?

HARRY. Oh don't be daft.

JENNY. What about me?

HARRY. Well that's it. That's what we got to talk about.

JENNY. What?

HARRY. Well she knows . . . for a start.

JENNY. I don't care. Corse she knows. That's what brings her running back. She thinks you're lying in a cold bed. She's punishing you.

HARRY. It's not like that.

JENNY. No? So where do I go?

HARRY. Look . . . I just want to give this marriage another chance. The kid, you know.

JENNY. You made me pregnant.

HARRY. I haven't.

JENNY. Yes.

HARRY. You told me it was alright.

JENNY. We all make mistakes.

HARRY. Blimey.

JENNY. Don't worry.

HARRY. Oh no. Well, we'll have to do something.

JENNY. Will we?

HARRY. Yes. I mean what I can to help.

JENNY. Like chucking me out of the house when you had enough.

HARRY. Jen . . . come on. Did I make any promises?

JENNY. No.

HARRY.   I'll help you. Course I will.

JENNY.   Ta.

HARRY.   Only . . .

JENNY.   I could have made that home pretty. I hated her taste. It's not cosy.
  But I wouldn't touch anything. I kept everything the way she left it. Only this
  week I saw some lovely material for the bedroom, the curtains . . . paisley.

HARRY.   These are alright, I think.

JENNY.   What?

HARRY.   The whatsaname. They're alright, aren't they — the ones up there?

JENNY.   Yeah. Get us another brandy love.

HARRY.   Sure. *(goes to bar.)* Brandy please, mate.

ANDREW.   One brandy.

HARRY.   When do you light the fires, Andrew?

ANDREW.   Twentieth of September.

ALBERT.   Even if there's a damn heatwave.

ANDREW.   Twentieth of September. Three shillings please.

ALBERT.   Everyone gets the right change then.

ANDREW.   Now then Albert, it is human to err. Thank you, sir.

HARRY.   Ta. *(He returns to table.)* Here y'are sir . . .

JENNY.   I thought in the winter . . . it could be nice. Do you want her back?

HARRY.   Don't know.

JENNY.   You could write and tell her not to come.

HARRY.   What's the point? Don't worry. Really I'm going to look after you.

JENNY.   Yes dear.

HARRY.   I suppose you, er . . . want a thing, do you?

JENNY.   Forty pound.

HARRY.   Forty pound? Yes? Is that good, is it?

JENNY.   Better than some.

HARRY.   I never seen you cry.

JENNY.   No.

HARRY.   This month has been marvellous. Look, if it doesn't work out with
  Ivy . . . I'm going to give it a try, but . . .

JENNY.   Yes I see. Where do I wait? Down the bottom of the garden? Don't
  be daft.

HARRY.   No. They say that dignity is in decision, you know.

JENNY.   Do they?

HARRY.   Existentialism.

JENNY.   Lovely, dear.

HARRY.   Oh Jen . . . am I a coward?

JENNY.   I think so. Never mind.

HARRY.   Some women would get hysterical, wouldn't they?

JENNY.   I don't know. Just don't go on, Harry. This isn't another story.

HARRY.   I've worked well while you've been in the house. Just — I wasn't
  bugged . . . and it worked. Why do I let this woman come back? Why? Why
  can't I let go?

JENNY.   Some people can't . . . some people can't get hold of anything. Let
  alone let go of it.

HARRY.   Oh Christ. I'm getting nervous already.

Sound of car arriving outside.

JENNY.   Can you get that money then?
HARRY.   Leave it to me.
JENNY.   I'm sorry.
HARRY.   Jen. Christ, girl.

IAN *comes in with* OSBORNE.

IAN.   Hi . . . Harry . . . Jen. Look Os.
OSBORNE.   Hello.
HARRY.   Evening.
IAN.   What's to be, Os old boy? *(*OSBORNE *gives* IAN *a note.)*
OSBORNE.   Er . . .
IAN.   Pints . . . three pints.
ANDREW.   Ordinary.
IAN.   Director's. Jen?
JENNY.   Brandy.
IAN.   One brandy. *(*OSBORNE *sits with* HARRY *and* JENNY.*)*
HARRY.   How's the religion then?
OSBORNE.   Don't get much time for it. Painting now. Ruth.
JENNY.   She lets you?
OSBORNE.   It's all well organised. Three hours a day. Heating very good.
   Coffee break. That's Ian's corner.
IAN.   Yeah. I get the blanket.
HARRY.   What?
IAN.   Round her shoulders. Break time.
OSBORNE.   Ian sees fair play . . . sort of.
IAN.   I'm the third man.
OSBORNE.   The second man.
IAN.   Sure.
JENNY.   What — is he there all the tiime?
OSBORNE.   When she's undressed. I prefer it. It's a solution . . . ideal. Room
   and board.
JENNY.   What?
OSBORNE.   Ian. For services rendered.
ANDREW *(calls over)*.   How are you, Mr Osborne?
OSBORNE.   Very well, thank you. Working hard.
ANDREW.   The fires.
OSBORNE.   What? When?
ALBERT.   Twentieth of September.
ANDREW.   I'll decide. Thank you very much, Albert. I'll decide.

IAN *brings drinks over and sits down.*

JENNY.   You moved in have you?
IAN.   Help. Cheers. Look after your sister. Keep it in the family.
JENNY.   Bastard.
IAN.   She's . . . He paints her well.
OSBORNE.   Thank you.
IAN.   No. That body . . . Ruth. You capture her.

OSBORNE. Do you think so?

IAN. Yeah.

OSBORNE. How is everything out here?

JENNY. As bloody awful as anywhere else.

OSBORNE. I'm not prying.

JENNY. Given up boredom for Lent, have you?

OSBORNE. Don't get much time for all that these days.

IAN. Yeah, Os . . . think . . . think.

OSBORNE. I beg your pardon?

IAN. Music.

OSBORNE. Yes?

IAN. Get a machine man . . . in the studio. L.P.

OSBORNE. Damned expensive.

IAN. Art.

OSBORNE. We'll discuss it later.

IAN. Sure. How's Ivy? Did I say something? Ah nuts. Forget it . . . life, man.

HARRY. What?

IAN. Continued.

HARRY. It'll take a few more drinks before mine picks up.

IAN. You got a problem.

HARRY. I won't have soon. Give it half an hour. Between boredom and despair . . . not much room.

IAN. Great. Let's enjoy.

HARRY. You're right. Sod it. To hell. Andrew — one brandy, three whiskies — Jesus Christ I get so angry.

IAN. Yeah.

HARRY. With myself.

IAN. Serious.

HARRY. It doesn't pay man. You're serious — you get crap. You're hilarious — you get crap.

IAN. Eat it.

HARRY. That's one way to get rid of it. *(Goes to counter.)*

IAN. Jen . . . *(Goes to touch her.)*

JENNY. Get off. You always get in somewhere, don't you?

IAN. What's the matter?

JENNY. You. *(Indicates HARRY.)* Him. *(Indicates OSBORNE.)* You can work it out between you, can't you?

IAN. Jen . . .

OSBORNE. What she's saying, Ian, is that it's a man's world.

JENNY. You belt up.

OSBORNE. You wouldn't speak like that if you were . . .

JENNY. If I had one of your horrible rooms . . . go on. Well I haven't. Stick it. I've always been rude to you.

OSBORNE. Yes.

JENNY. Keeping both of 'em now are you . . . in sin?

OSBORNE. Sin . . . it needs a tremendous amount of reflection to even dabble.

IAN. Oh . . . yeah.

HARRY *(brings drinks back)*. Darts?

OSBORNE.   Yes. *(OSBORNE goes to the board with HARRY.)*
HARRY.   Be my guest. Chinese style tonight, what? You hold the dart and
   I throw the board at it.
JENNY.   Ivy's coming back.
IAN *(they are alone at table)*.   Yeah. You been there
JENNY.   Eh?
IAN.   Collect.
JENNY.   He's not a rat like you.
IAN.   You want help?
JENNY.   Yes.
IAN.   Come to me.
JENNY.   You don't believe.
IAN.   Oh Jen . . . that. Be fair. I wronged you. Don't turn the con . . . on me.
   Listen . . . you operate . . . OK. Don't cut me in . . . OK, OK. I'm not
   mean. Collect from Harry. He's had you a month. Forty stinking pounds
   — what's that?
JENNY.   You should be paying that.
IAN.   You want eighty.
JENNY.   You did it, not him. *(HARRY has come back and overheard.)*
HARRY.   You going to take chalks Ian?
IAN.   Sure.

Scene 3

Postscript. End of season.
Farmhouse kitchen.
IAN *having lunch with* HARRY *and* IVY *They are finishing a meal. Door*
open. Sun pours through.

HARRY.   More wine? *(Pours it.)*
IAN.   Last supper.
IVY.   What time you leaving for London?
IAN.   Tomorrow. With the vegetables . . . lift. I got to help load on — five in
   the morning . . . roll on.
HARRY.   London.
IAN.   Got any friends in London? I'll look 'em up.
HARRY.   No thanks.
IAN.   Sure . . . you know. I think so.
HARRY.   What?
IAN.   Look her up.
IVY.   I'll put the coffee on. *(She goes to prepare the coffee.)*
HARRY.   Jen?
IAN.   Great little fixer.
HARRY.   Had me fooled.
IAN.   Sure . . . you know what I mean.
HARRY.   Course I do. Why don't you tell me?
IAN.   Knew how to handle herself.
HARRY.   Ivy's not interested, are you darling?

IVY.   Carry on, don't mind me. I don't mind her living here rent free. But when she tries to leave with forty pounds . . .

IAN.   Look . . . listen. Ivy . . . you don't work in these stinking restaurants . . .

IVY.   I have done.

IAN.   You're lucky. Harry. Play on at the Royal Court. What's it about.

HARRY.   Well it's not about us.

IVY.   She would take people for all she could get.

HARRY.   They all do. Ivy. Women. Cling. There must be a basic economic relationship between us, Ivy.

IVY.   It's about time we had one.

HARRY.   Alright dear . . . look, sex . . . look how happy we've been since the money started coming in. Wine on the table. Punch-up about three times a week. I mean, things are improving all the time.

IVY.   I earn more than you've ever paid me. Bleedin' socialist. Don't mind exploiting your wife, do you?

HARRY.   Certainly not. I could not exploit a nicer person.

POSTMAN *appears in doorway.*

POSTMAN.   Posty. Parcel — Mr Ian Bellmore, care of here.

HARRY.   I'll see he gets it.

POSTMAN.   Lovely day. Lovely day. *(Going.)* Lovely day. Lovely day.

HARRY *brings parcel to table.* IVY *brings coffee over.*

HARRY.   Bit of luck.

IAN.   Who's it from?

HARRY.   Jennifer Robinson. Jen.

IAN *(undoes parcel)*. Hey . . . see. That bird. My birthday last week. I was upset. She forgot. True love . . . Jen. You can't forget her.

Opens parcel. Recoils in horror. HARRY *and* IVY *look into parcel. Sick.*

Scene 4

Pub.
Evening.
ANDREW *and* ALBERT *alone.*

ANDREW.   And then I had to shave her.

ALBERT.   Shave her?

ANDREW.   Yes.

ALBERT.   Who?

ANDREW.   You know.

ALBERT.   The unmentionable object.

ANDREW.   You will not take my wife's name in vain.

ALBERT.   I will not mention her.

ANDREW.   And then I changed the blade.

ALBERT.   Why did you do it?

ANDREW. The lather.
ALBERT. That?
ANDREW. Oh yes.
ALBERT. And did you use . . .
ANDREW. What. You don't think I can afford a new brush do you, three times a week?
ALBERT. Three times a week.
ANDREW. I changed the blade. I wouldn't use the same blade.
ALBERT. Because of the hormones.
ANDREW. Because of the bloody principle, man. Would you care to see the razor?
ALBERT. That razor?
ANDREW. Aye.

ANDREW *undoes his tie and unbuttons shirt. Tied to a string round his neck is a key. Opens little wooden box and produces razor.*

ALBERT. Oh . . . phew. I wouldn't mind a shave with that, Andrew.
ANDREW. Don't drink too much tonight.
ALBERT. I see. What did you do with the blade?
ANDREW *(Puts razor away).* I put them in the disposer?
ALBERT. What did you do with the disposer?
ANDREW. I disposed of it. You're sailing close to the wind tonight.
ALBERT. I know.
ANDREW. You know that Alf . . .
ALBERT. Alf?
ANDREW. Alf is dead.
ALBERT. Oh no.
ANDREW. I went to his basket. He hadn't been out for about three weeks. The food was littering the kitchen. Stinking.
ALBERT. So you looked in the basket.
ANDREW. Only thing. Pluck up the nerve. Dead as a doornail.
ALBERT. Why did you wait till now to tell me?
ANDREW. I wanted to show you the razor first. *(Sound of car drawing up.)* Don't tell anyone.
ALBERT. No.
ANDREW. Never. Keep up appearances.
ALBERT. They'll miss him.
ANDREW. Not as much as I do.

Curtain.

UP IN THE HIDE

Characters

BILL, *the white hunter*
LILLY, *a journalist*
ROBERT, *her husband*
MR DIMITRY, *an American tourist*
MRS DIMITRY, *his wife*
FLANAGAN, *a film star*
TESSA, *his wife*
FRED, *a businessman*
MICHAEL (*aka* EMMA), *his personal assistant*
PIKE, *a mercenary*
UMBOKO, SUBABA, *servants*

First night at the Gate Theatre, London, 17th April 1980. Directed by Lou Stein. Designed by Wallace Helm and Jim Daly.

BILL	Mike McKevitt
UMBOKO	Burt Caesar
SUBABA	Brian Bovell
PIKE	James Fleet
DORIS DIMITRY	Costance Reason
WILMUR DIMITRY	Arthur Nightingale
FLANAGAN	Peter Stenson
TESSA	Lizza Aiken
LILLY LANGTON	Pam Mettick
ROBERT LANGTON	Carl Forgione
FRED	Mike Burnside
MICHAEL	Brendan Murray

ACT ONE

Scene 1

It is really a rather grand bamboo hut . . . somewhere in the veld. There is an observation window upstage with a sort of gauze to keep the mosquitoes out. The room we see is large, filling the stage, with doors either side — flimsy, and with more of the gauze stuff in the upper panels. There is another door upstage leading to the kitchen and servants' quarters. Perhaps the observation window is on a raised gallery with steps either side — just a few feet higher than ground level. The lounge furniture might be bamboo — glass topped tables — magazines lying about — a couple of leopard- or tiger-skin rugs. Perhaps some wall mountings — horns sort of thing. The place is done up to impress — lots of jungle atmosphere — in case no animals turn up to be observed. What we have is a commercial concern bringing tourists to observe and photograph (they hope) the animals of Rhodesia. Actually it's all a bit tatty. The servants are all coloured — which does add to the atmosphere.

When the lights come up on the scene (or the curtain rises), LILLY is seated, flicking through some magazines. She is rather attractive, about thirty years old, and has managed to fashion a costume straight out of the Somerset Maugham era . . . which somehow looks quite modern.

BILL enters, the white hunter. In his early fifties. Khaki shorts and drill. Not very smart. I suppose he looks quite fit, but whisky has been doing some inside work on his system. He raises his head as he enters the room, instinctively sensing where everybody is . . . in this case LILLY. He relaxes and goes to the observation window. Lights up pipe.

LILLY becomes aware of him.

LILLY. Good evening . . . where does one get a drink round here?
BILL. Ring the bell . . .
LILLY. There isn't one . . .
BILL. It should be on the table . . . (LILLY *looks round, without getting up.*) No?
LILLY. Not here . . .
BILL. Then he's hidden it . . . (BILL *stares out of the observation window. After a few minutes* LILLY *decides to pursue the matter.*)
LILLY. Who?
BILL. Mmmm . . . ?
LILLY. Who has hidden it?

BILL.   Umboko ... *(Long pause.)* They do as they like ... *(Making himself more explicit.)* The boys ...

LILLY.   You still call them boys do you?

BILL.   Don't think about it ...

LILLY.   Did Mister Flanagan get here?

BILL.   Not yet ...

LILLY.   Is he lost?

BILL.   Possibly ... Hope so ... That would scare the blighter eh ... It's alright, I know this place like Oxford Street ... *(Longer pause.)* Mind you I don't know Oxford Street — these days ...

LILLY.   Is it safe out there? With all the animals?

BILL.   You're being hopeful ... All what animals?

LILLY.   They were on the brochure ...

BILL.   Yes ... Well he's probably frightened them all away by now ... lumbering around out there in the dark ...

LILLY.   It's funny ... I was after Richard O'Flanagan in England ... some time back ... for an article ... Well I never got to him ... he was ill and wouldn't see anyone ... I hate it when I can't get my feature articles ... when I can't get the subject I want ... *(Opens magazine.)* I don't know that I'm so interested now ... *(Pause — reflects.)* Well I am ...

BILL *(pause)*.   What are you? A doctor?

LILLY.   No — a journalist ...

BILL.   I thought you said he was ill ... ?

LILLY.   He was ...

BILL.   And you were trying to get to him ... ? I don't understand ... *(Returns to staring out of the window.)*

LILLY.   Don't we get a drink? After sundown? Don't we get a famous sundowner? It's pitch dark outside isn't it?

BILL.   Catches them unawares ...

LILLY.   What?

BILL.   The boys ... They can't mix the cocktails in time ... the sun's gone down before they get the ice in ...

Enter UMBOKO, *with tray bearing cocktail flask and glasses.*

UMBOKO.   Here'y'are Daddy ... this is the cocktail hour ...

BILL.   Thank you Umboko ...

UMBOKO *(mildly derisive)*.   Shall I pour? Shall I roll my eyes?

BILL.   No thank you Umboko, that will be all ...

UMBOKO *(bows — sending the whole thing up)*.   Thank you Sa'ab ... *(He leaves.)*

BILL *(pours the drinks)*.   Difficult to get a good boy these days ...

LILLY.   Well he seemed alright ...

BILL.   Did you think so? I thought he was rather ... sending the whole thing up?

LILLY.   Oh it's quite common ...

BILL.   What, even in London?

LILLY.   Oh yes ... Waiters always send you up in London ... it's part of the game ...

BILL *(thoughtfully)*.   Ohh ... *(hands her drink.)* Cheers ...

LILLY.   Bungho . . .

BILL.   Down the hatch . . . *(They drink.)* Let's have another.

LILLY *(surprised).*   I haven't finished this one yet . . .

BILL *(whose glass is empty).*   Let me top it up . . . *(He fills glasses again.)*

LILLY.   Have you got a history? I suppose you must have?

BILL.   Oh yes . . . Bomber pilot . . .

LILLY.   First of the Few?

BILL.   No no . . . there were more of us . . . Bombers . . . not fighters . . . we weren't the Few . . . Mind you there weren't so many of us left at the end . . .

LILLY.   Are you English?

BILL.   Oh yes — I emigrated . . . God knows why . . . Couldn't go back . . . Like a jungle back there — London . . . Traffic — every time I go back there I get run over . . . I've learnt my lesson . . . Strip clubs — out as far as Penge by now I hear . . . No I shan't go back . . . It was a bus last time . . . It was an awful lesson to me . . . I didn't know they ran at that time of night . . .

LILLY.   Was it an all night bus?

BILL.   Must have been . . . didn't see it coming . . . nasty brute . . . got me outside The Owl and The Pussycat . . .

LILLY.   Where are the others?

BILL.   Changing . . . The Americans take a long while changing . . . It's like a costume set-piece to them . . . I don't know where they get their outfits . . . they're like Hollywood job lots . . .

Enter two Americans, MR *and* MRS DIMITRY. *They are very Stewart Granger and Ava Gardner . . . He being a retired mortician taking his wife on the trip he'd always promised her.*

MR DIMITRY.   Hello there! Is it time for drinkies? Has the sun gone down? I must say it's quick around these parts!

MRS DIMITRY.   Weren't we going to see the animals at the pool? At sundown? Wilmer?

MR DIMITRY.   Right outside the window Doris . . .

MRS DIMITRY.   But it's pitch black out there . . .

BILL.   We got out here a bit late Mrs Dimitry . . . Trouble with the Landrover don't you know . . .

MRS DIMITRY.   Three hours . . . three hours stuck in that thing . . . in the blazing heat . . .

BILL.   Drink?

MRS DIMITRY.   Lemonade please . . . *(*MRS DIMITRY *looks fed up.)*

MR DIMITRY.   Similar . . .

MRS DIMITRY.   Why don't you service your trucks out here?

BILL.   It's very difficult to get spare parts . . . There's a trade embargo . . .

MRS DIMITRY.   Don't tell me about politics . . . I don't want to know about that . . . I came here to see the animals and it's pitch dark out there . . . Have you brought the flash? *(*MR and MRS DIMITRY *both have cameras round their necks.)*

MR DIMITRY.   Yes Doris . . .

MRS DIMITRY.   You bring plenty of new film? *(*BILL *finds the small hand bell under the table. He rings it.)*

MR DIMITRY.   Uhhuh . . .

MRS DIMITRY.   Is that a new film you got in the camera?

MR DIMITRY.   Errr . . . well I think I might have a couple of Sir Laurence on it . . . Say what gives with you English types? We're down your National Theatre right . . . the Old Vic is that it . . .

MRS DIMITRY.   That's right . . .

MR DIMITRY.   And they got a sign up . . . no photographs to be taken during the performance . . . what the hell we go there for? Anyway we got him . . .

MRS DIMITRY.   We got him alright . . .

MR DIMITRY.   We got him with the handkerchief . . . we got him with Desdemona . . . we caught him! He looked really angry didn't he Doris?

MRS DIMITRY.   Who? Sir Larry?

MR DIMITRY.   Yeah . . .

MRS DIMITRY.   Oh that wasn't at you . . . that was at Desdemona . . . that was good acting that's all that was . . .

MR DIMITRY.   Well that's alright then . . . Anyway we got something to show the children . . .

Enter UMBOKO.

BILL.   Two lemonades Umboko . . .

UMBOKO.   You going on the wagon sir?

BILL.   No I'm not . . .

UMBOKO.   I didn't think you was . . . *(He leaves.)*

BILL.   Cheeky bugger . . . I can't get used to that sort of thing . . .

MRS DIMITRY.   Are they dangerous?

BILL (*still looking at door where* UMBOKO *has gone out*).   Hard to say yet . . .

MR DIMITRY (*getting* BILL's *attention*).   My wife says are the animals dangerous?

BILL.   Ohh them . . . No . . . not unless you provoke them . . .

MRS DIMITRY.   Provoke them? What does that mean?

BILL.   Well they don't like being photographed — too much — like Sir Laurence . . .

MR DIMITRY.   I told you he was angry . . .

MRS DIMITRY.   That was at Desdemona . . .

MR DIMITRY.   Then why was he looking at me . . . *(To* LILLY.*)* Oh hello . . . Good evening . . . my name is Mr Dimitry and this is my wife Mrs Dimitry — the Second . . . How are you? I hope you're well . . . *(*LILLY *extends her hand.* MR DIMITRY *takes it.* MRS DIMITRY *has gone up to the observation platform and is peering out.)*

MRS DIMITRY.   Is it alright talking so loud? Shouldn't we be talking in whispers?

BILL.   No the animals are as at home as if they were in err — Grand Central Park . . . They're used to the nasal twang and the err — comments while they drink . . . but they don't like the flash . . . we all have to take the flash together . . . because they hoof it . . .

LILLY.   Rather like the National! *(Explaining more.)* Theatre . . .

MR DIMITRY.   Oh yeah . . . *(Thinks.)* I don't know about . . . They weren't so keen on Mrs Dimitry's comments either . . . they were most flattering . . . I mean even if Sir Laurence heard what she was saying — it was only praise . . . I would have thought he'd have been encouraged to act even harder . . . Encouragement is what we all need . . .

LILLY.   Yes . . . 'Go on Sir Larry! You're doing well tonight!'

MR DIMITRY (*doubtfully*).   Well . . . (MR DIMITRY *moves upstage. UMBOKO enters with tray. MR DIMITRY takes the two lemonades.*) Thank you Umboko. (*UMBOKO shakes the tray above his head and bangs it with his fist.*)

UMBOKO.   Helleluhiah!

MR DIMITRY.   Yeah — well we get a lot of that . . .

UMBOKO *exits.* MR DIMITRY *takes the lemonade onto observation platform where his wife is peering out of window.*

BILL.   Where's your husband?

LILLY.   Writing . . .

BILL.   Ahh . . . I thought you were on holiday?

LILLY.   We are . . . for six months he couldn't write, so we decide to take a holiday . . . Now he's writing . . . He writes at Christmas when we have visitors . . . He writes when I have babies . . . When I need him, he's writing . . . most of the time I don't need him — he can't put down a word . . . Six hundred pounds we paid for this trip . . . so that he can sit in a darkened room in the middle of Africa and type . . . I knew it would happen — Bill — it is Bill isn't it?

BILL.   How did you know?

LILLY.   Well you're the Bill type . . .

BILL.   Amazing . . .

LILLY.   I said to Larry . . .

BILL.   Olivier?

LILLY.   No my husband Larry . . . 'I might as well shut you up in the bathroom — we don't need to go to Africa . . . We could have had the taps running and we could have put on a record of jungle noises . . .'

BILL.   Well — if it's a new novel he's writing that should pay for the trip . . .

LILLY (*silent a moment*).   It's my articles pay for the trip . . .

BILL.   He might sell the film rights . . . they do you know . . .

LILLY.   He has to finish it first . . . (*She seems bitter.*) Never mind . . . (*As she turns another page of the magazine.*) Did you get these magazines from a dentist's waiting room? (*Pause — rather worried.*) I didn't want to come here you know . . . I've got a regular column in the best Sunday . . . now some brat of a girl's taken it over for a month . . . She's bound to be brilliant — they always are . . . Cockney rebel . . . Oh I shall get back . . . I always do . . . tough as old boots . . . that's me . . . But it hurts to let my space go to some illiterate bitch . . . who will charm the pants off 'em with her confessions of prick teasing the personalities . . . It's not objective is it? It's not objective reporting . . . I put myself in the picture — they like that — but I don't take their trousers off . . .

BILL.   Who?

LILLY.   The men I'm sent to hunt down . . .

BILL.   Well you've got Flanagan haven't you? You were after him . . . Isn't that what you call a scoop? You'll have him all to yourself . . . If the lions haven't eaten him . . .

LILLY.   He's overexposed . . . You've got to get him on the raw to get a good
story . . . I tried to get into the mental home where he was — when he was ill
. . . but those wretched nuns were all over the place . . . I think they hid him
somewhere . . . It's being exposed to the public and the press makes them ill
you know . . . Somebody like Flanagan . . .

BILL.   I should have thought your job was to make the boring interesting . . .
you could even do a good job on me you know . . . perhaps not . . . They think
I'm a character — some sort of renegade . . . I'm only a tourist guide really . . .
I mean if I was in Austria I'd be done up in leather shorts wouldn't I — leading
them up and down mountains . . . We're all in the same business . . . there's
no romance in my life . . .

LILLY.   Were you ever married?

BILL.   No . . . avoid it like the plague . . . I've seen too much of it . . . I've seen
what it does to people . . . It's not natural you know . . . that's my conclusion
. . . marriage . . . *(He pauses.)*

LILLY *(encourages him)*.   Go on . . .

BILL.   You get a lot of it out here now . . . I see it at close quarters . . . married
couples . . . on these weekend safaris . . . It can be quite savage *(Waves at
window.)* I look out of the window . . . I mind my own business . . . *(Listens.)*
Hello — here comes the other Landrover . . .

LILLY *(straining to hear)*.   Can you hear it?

BILL.   Smell it . . . *(Sound of Landrover approaching.)*

LILLY.   You're right . . . Prepare for boarders . . .

There are chairs up on the observation platfrom, so that MR *and* MRS
DIMITRY *have made themselves quite comfortable.*

MRS DIMITRY.   Wilmer — I hear something outside. Can you see anything?

MR DIMITRY.   No . . .

MRS DIMITRY.   Quite definitely there is something . . .

MR DIMITRY.   I'm not disputing it . . . You know Doris I think I'll have a
little something in my lemonade next time . . . I'm not going to go behind
your back . . .

MRS DIMITRY.   Ssshhh . . . Listen . . . *(There is a sort of growling roar
outside.)* Quick Wilmer! Shoot it! *(They both fire their flash cameras. The
growl outside becomes a human laugh.)*

MR DIMITRY.   Well I'll be darned! That was a humanoid!

MRS DIMITRY.   Is that what we pay fifteen-hundred dollars for?

MR DIMITRY.   Certainly not Doris . . . I promised you the best . . . This is
your retirement present! You know who that was you just photographed?
Mr Flanagan! Now he's a star in his own right . . .

MRS DIMITRY.   I never heard of him . . . *(Different sort of animal noise
now.)* I didn't come here to take photographs of Mr Flanagan fooling around
. . . That won't mean nothing to the children . . .

Enter FLANAGAN *in open-neck shirt and slacks, looking quite civilised. A
pair of binoculars round his neck. He is about forty to fifty years old. Handsome.
There is something rather wild about him. With binoculars to his eyes he creeps
up on* MRS DIMITRY.

FLANAGAN.   Bearer . . . Bring me my rifle . . . I've spotted an American heiress . . . my God she's beautiful . . . It's the heat . . . the heat playing tricks with my emotions . . . *(Goes down on his knees in front of her.)* Marry me . . . You won't regret it . . . Not for a week . . .

MR DIMITRY.   Now hold on . . .

FLANAGAN *(leaps up)*.   Who are you sir? That you have this lady in thrall! I'll break your spell damn you! She's mine! Mine! Down to the last arthritic bone!

MR DIMITRY.   Doris you won't see a performance like that outside the National . . .

FLANAGAN.   And it's free . . . Cocktails! Quickly! Umboko! Where is that man? Where is that black scoundrel?!

UMBOKO *(enters)*.   Here I is masser . . .

FLANAGAN.   I'll have the hide off you! Now then none of your Mau Mau rituals . . . Get us a drink . . . Quick . . . !

UMBOKO.   You get me on your show sometime?

FLANAGAN.   If you pay your own fare back to England . . .

UMBOKO.   England? Who goes there any more . . . *(He leaves.)*

Enter SUBABA *with luggage. Followed by* FRED *and* EMMA. FRED *is about fifty-five years old, a bit camp in his new clothes.* EMMA *is a twenty-year-old young man, who is beautiful; he is not really camp, but can put it on if it suits him to flirt.*

FRED.   Is this it? Emma is this it?

EMMA.   Why do you need me to tell you . . .

FRED.   I need you to tell me everything . . . That's what you're paid for . . . So this is it?

EMMA.   Yes . . . And the name's Michael not Emma . . . It's too early for Emma . . .

FRED.   Sorry . . . Well as my private secretary can you tell me is this it? Have we come to the right address?

EMMA.   You've been drinking too much . . .

FRED.   Isn't this a holiday? I'm pleading with you . . . Michael?

EMMA.   Yes it's a holiday . . .

FRED.   Thank you . . . Thank you . . .

FLANAGAN.   Oh stop quarrelling you two . . .

BILL.   Where's your wife Mr Flanagan?

FLANAGAN.   Oh she fell off about a mile back . . .

BILL.   Fell off?

FLANAGAN.   Oh yes . . . she would sit with her feet over the tail board . . .

BILL.   Why didn't you tell somebody she fell off?

FLANAGAN.   Didn't seem important . . .

BILL.   This is rough country Mr Flanagan . . .

FLANAGAN.   Ohh it pays to advertise . . .

SUBABA *is bringing in more luggage.* BILL *addresses him in Swahili (or something that sounds like African). The conversation is short and urgent.* BILL *and* SUBABA *exit.*

FLANAGAN.   Are they looking for her? Pity . . . I'd call that an act of God . . . I don't think you should interfere with that . . .

MRS DIMITRY.   Mr Flanagan, it's not wise to leave your wife outside in this sort of country . . .

FLANAGAN.   Oh no . . . Thanks for the tip Belle . . . What time's this steamer get into Los Angeles? *(*UMBOKO *brings in more drinks.)* Ahh here comes Heart of Darkness . . . Been counting your skulls out there have you? Don't pay attention to me . . . I'm the same with the Irish . . . and the Jews . . .

MRS DIMITRY.   Did you hear that?

MR DIMITRY.   Why should *we* worry?

FRED.   Michael this is your idea . . .

EMMA.   I wanted to get out of Nairobi . . .

FRED.   I don't think it's a good idea that we're thrown so much upon each other's company . . .

EMMA.   I wanted to get out of the flat . . .

FRED.   And away from the bars? I heard someone was after you with a knife . . ? Is that right . . ? (*Whispers.*) You ungrateful wretch . . .

UMBOKO *exits.*

FLANAGAN.   Have the Press arrived? Yes . . .

LILLY.   I am on holiday Mr Flanagan . . . I shan't be seeking an interview with you . . . I'm not writing this month . . .

FLANAGAN.   Ohh we are playing hard to get . . . Lilly Langtry isn't it?

LILLY.   Langton . . .

FLANAGAN.   Lilly Lally? Isn't that your absurd pen name? Haven't I seen your name on the book stalls? Haven't you been signing copies in Harrods because you can't pay your account? Aren't you enjoying a modest success Miss Langton?

LILLY (*quite pleased that he knows so much*).   I am . . . And if you decide to be pleasant for the next thirty-six hours we'll all have a much nicer time . . .

FLANAGAN.   Where's your hubby?

LILLY.   Typing . . .

FLANAGAN.   Don't you mean writing?

LILLY.   Whatever . . .

FLANAGAN.   Noel Langton? Are his books on the stalls? Didn't he have a huge success . . . ?

LILLY.   Twelve years ago . . . Did you read his book on the civil war?

FLANAGAN.   Which one?

LILLY.   The English one . . . It was very — definitive . . .

FLANAGAN.   Good . . . Look here you don't have to pull the wool over my eyes . . . You're keeping the old man with your little jottings . . . That's alright by me . . . Someone's got to keep the wolf from the door . . . It's when its tearing at your heart . . . Poor man — hasn't he had any . . .

LILLY.   Two books . . . but they did nothing . . . since the civil war thing . . . He's getting desperate . . . I'm afraid . . .

FLANAGAN.   Course he's getting desperate . . . Wouldn't you get desperate? Well isn't there another book in Cromwell?

LILLY.   No . . . He's tried thrillers recently . . .

FLANAGAN. Cookery's the best bet . . . Why can't he write a book on cookery in the civil war? Seventeen-hundred . . . When was it?

LILLY. He's a very good cook . . .

FLANAGAN. I bet he is . . . With you out at all hours . . . Interviewing . . . Is he a pinafore type is he? Have you broken his spirit? Have you crept up on him? With your meagre talents . . . Were they enough to win the day?

LILLY. Robert's problems are of his own making . . . I've tried encouraging him . . .

FLANAGAN. Yes you used to admire him . . . but you've wriggled out of that one . . . How to tame an author . . . So all his plots are about men who murder their wives . . . ?

LILLY. Yes . . .

FLANAGAN. I'm not surprised . . . He'll find the perfect answer . . .

TESSA *comes in. She is about twenty-three. She slaps* FLANAGAN's *face.*

TESSA. You beast! You pushed me off! *(She exits — through to inner rooms.)*

FLANAGAN. I married an idiot . . . She won't have children in case it ruins her figure . . . I slipped up there . . .

LILLY. You were very silly pushing her off the back of that truck . . .

FLANAGAN. Well we weren't discussing anything very important . . . I mean you're the fecund one aren't you? How many kiddies have you got?

LILLY. Three . . .

FLANAGAN. Yes they're always featured in your column . . . little brats . . . about how they can't shit poperly and you hold them upside down . . .

LILLY. I'm glad you read my column . . .

FLANAGAN. Well I can't concentrate . . . I read anything . . . I quite like how you destroy people you get near . . . it makes good reading . . . Did you just start writing to revenge yourself on your husband? Or was there some ulterior motive?

BILL (*marches in*). That was a damn silly thing to do sir . . . Push your wife off the back of a truck . . .

FLANAGAN. She slipped . . .

BILL. You should still have reported it . . .

FLANAGAN. I was going to . . . At roll-call . . .

BILL. To the driver . . .

FLANAGAN. He doesn't speak English . . .

BILL. You should have shouted and pointed . . .

FLANAGAN. It hardly seemed worth it . . . We were nearly here . . .

BILL. This is a damn dangerous country sir . . .

FLANAGAN. Well that's what we paid for . . . isn't it?

BILL. And how did you get lost?

FLANAGAN. I persuaded the driver to go looking for elephants . . .

BILL. He arrived here with an empty petrol tank . . .

FLANAGAN. I'm trying to add a little bit of zest to our holiday . . .

BILL. I am responsible for your safety . . .

FLANAGAN. Then who is responsible for our danger? After all this is supposed to be a holiday with a difference isn't it? Shouldn't the lights fail or something and we start murdering each other . . . You should really be off your nut you know . . . You should be a tyrant of some sort . . . Surely something happens late at night when you've had a few whiskies . . . Or is it all down to wife swapping *à la* on the veld . . . 'Cos we could have stayed in Croydon for that . . . *(To* LILLY*)* Couldn't we ducky?

LILLY.   I didn't think you lived in Croydon . . . I thought it was Epsom . . .

FLANAGAN.   No that's my private mental home . . . West Hampstead is the place where I really go mad . . . that's Home . . .

BILL.   Damn silly thing . . . all this mucking about . . . Now let's all settle down . . . *(Rings bell.* UMBOKO *enters.)* Umboko . . .

UMBOKO.   What you want guv?

BILL.   Is the television working? What's on tonight?

UMBOKO.   No telly out here tonight . . . All the valves is gone . . .

BILL.   Gone?

UMBOKO.   Vanished . . . *(He leaves.)*

BILL *(calls after him).*   More drinks . . . *(More generally.)* Then we'll all get cleaned up for dinner shall we?

MRS DIMITRY.   When do we see the animals?

BILL.   At dawn . . . I want you all to have an early night . . . That's what we've come out for . . . Half of them sleep through it . . . Not bad for six hundred pounds . . .

MR DIMITRY.   You be sure to call us . . .

MRS DIMITRY.   Oh I'll set the alarm Wilmer . . .

BILL.   No alarms . . . We must be very quiet . . .

MR DIMITRY *(to* MRS DIMITRY*).*   You hear that? No alarm clocks . . . No early morning calls . . .

MRS DIMITRY.   I shan't sleep . . . I want my money's worth . . .

BILL.   Umboko will call you . . .

MRS DIMITRY.   He's not creeping into my room . . . No thank you . . .

MR DIMITRY.   Doris . . .

MRS DIMITRY.   Now you shut up Wilmer . . . They're going to take over in this country the same as they have back home . . . If they can win in the bedrooms they'll defeat us . . .

MR DIMITRY.   Nonesense . . .

FRED.   What time is dinner? Excuse me . . . *(To* EMMA*.)* Ask them what time dinner is . . .

EMMA.   You've already asked them . . .

FRED.   Yes that was a mistake . . . I'm asking you to ask them . . . I'm pleading with you . . . Do it as a sign of trust . . .

EMMA.   What time is dinner please . . . ?

BILL.   Eight o'clock . . .

FRED.   Thank you . . . *(To* EMMA*).* Thank you . . . *(Overwrought, he takes out hanky.)* Thank you very much . . . *(Hurries out — pausing at door to make a last accusation to* EMMA*.)* Was that too much to ask? *(He exits.)*

FLANAGAN.   What's wrong with old Fred?

EMMA.   Nothing . . . he's always like that . . . I have to demonstrate my affection . . . I have to tell him the time — often . . . I have to ask useless questions of strangers . . . and when I carry these titbits of information back to him . . .

FLANAGAN.   He bursts into tears . . . Have you tried telling him more than the time?

EMMA.   Why should I? That's what I'm paid to do . . .

FRED *(Appears in doorway — tearful).*   I know what the time is . . . I just want to know what time dinner is . . . You are my private secretary Michael . . . I'm only asking you to fulfil a function aren't I — dear boy . . .

BILL.   Dinner is at eight sir . . .

FRED.   Why can't he tell me? What am I paying for . . .

FRED *exits.* UMBOKO *enters. Serves more drinks.*

BILL.   Mr Flanagan I'd be most interested to hear about your career . . . at first hand . . . I've seen several of your films . . . You're quite well known . . . even in Rhodesia . . . *(Waits for an answer. Doesn't get one.)* Do you get nervous in front of the cameras? I should imagine you would . . . Perhaps not . . . You're not much help are you? I don't have to make conversation . . .

FLANAGAN.   I thought you did . . .

BILL.   No . . .

FLANAGAN.   My mistake . . . You're very good at it . . .

BILL.   Find me a bit tame do you? I should be risking life and limb for you . . . warding off the snarls in the night . . . Well you learn a few things out here you know . . .

FLANAGAN.   Now this is what I've wanted to hear . . .

LILLY *(softly).*   Pig . . .

BILL.   I know one thing that'll kill a man . . . *(Holds up his glass.)* Whisky . . . I've seen it . . . *(He moves away — towards the* DIMITRYS.*)* Are you enjoying the trip?

MRS DIMITRY.   No . . . I came here to see animals . . . not to be bitten by mosquitoes . . .

BILL.   Haven't you put the repellant on?

MRS DIMITRY.   What repellant?

MR DIMITRY *(brings out small bottle).*   Oh sorry . . .

MRS DIMITRY.   If there's repellant I should be wearing it . . .

MR DIMITRY.   Oh sorry . . . I thought . . . Well honey with all the other stuff you put on that would repel 'em enough . . . *(Laughs weakly.)* Sorry honey . . . I plain forgot . . . *(She snatches the bottle and applies contents to her skin.)*

MRS DIMITRY.   You didn't forget to put it on yourself . . . Do you want me to die of malaria?

MR DIMITRY.   No dear . . .

MRS DIMITRY.   Well what do you want me to die of?

MR DIMITRY.   I don't want you to die of anything . . . *(To* BILL*)* And you're my witness . . .

BILL.   What is your calling back home sir?

MR DIMITRY.   Mortician . . .

BILL.   My goodness . . .

MR DIMITRY.   I've seen some beautiful people . . .

MRS DIMITRY.   He could make the devil look lovely laid out . . .

MR DIMITRY. Thank you ... thank you Doris ... a compliment in season ...

MRS DIMITRY (*slaps herself*). They're still biting me ...

BILL. Put more on ... We've gallons of it about ...

FLANAGAN. If there was a bus back tonight I'd take it ...

LILLY. And me ... Don't you like the Wild Life? Aren't you trying to save it? This is one of your causes Mr Flanagan ...

FLANAGAN. I'm trying to save myself at the moment Lilly ... from a marriage I should never have entered into ... to a very, very stupid woman ... I thought she was playing dumb ... I was convinced it was an act ... (ROBERT *enters. Goes up to* LILLY.)

ROBERT. I've stopped ...

LILLY. Stopped writing? You were doing so well ...

FLANAGAN. Try Mongolia ... Try going there ... You might start again ...

ROBERT. I try to write too well ... So then I thought the answer was cheap work ... But it bores me ... (*Takes drink from* UMBOKO.) Thank you ... If it bores me it's going to bore everybody else ...

LILLY. Did you have to come to Africa to find out that? (*Softer.*) Never mind, pet ... It was worth it ...

ROBERT. What am I going to do now ... ?

LILLY. Have a holiday Robert ...

Scene 2

The room is empty. Until BILL *comes in. He looks worried and is holding a type-written list. He is now wearing something resembling mess-kit (R.A.F.)*

BILL. Where's the Pikes? I've got the Pikes on my list ... (*Shouts*) Subaba! Subaba! (SUBABA *enters. Speaks African.*) Where are the Pikes? The honeymoon couple? (*Attempts this in African.* SUBABA *answers in African.*) You left them in bed ... They wouldn't come ... ? You're sure they haven't been eaten? (*Puts this in African.* SUBABA *shakes his head.*) Right ... They're on the list you see ... They shouldn't be on the list if they're not coming ... You could have counted them on the list ... you could have counted the numbers ... (SUBABA *takes the list. Takes out pencil and crosses out their names. Gives list back to* BILL. SUBABA *speaks African.*) Yes ... Well that's not very official but it will do ... (*Reads out.*) Mr and Mrs Flanagan ... Mr and Mrs Dimitry ... Mr and Mrs Langton ... Mr F. Proud and Michael Font ... All present and correct ... Now it's just a matter of keeping this lot alive till the dawn chorus ... You see Subaba it's because it is so undangerous — that it becomes dangerous ... Am I shouting at you? Sorry ... They can't see any animals around so they really assume there aren't any. Why am I carrying this revolver?

SUBABA. The emergency ... African terrorists ...

BILL (*giving him an old fashioned look*). Yes ... Well it's not affecting the tourist trade is it? Yet ... Are all the beds made?

SUBABA. Yes Bill . . .

BILL. Why do you make me speak to you in African half the time?

SUBABA. Half and half . . . We have a national language . . . You do well to learn it . . . *(He leaves.)*

BILL. *(mutters as he goes).* Yes . . . New Prime Minister I wouldn't wonder . . . Still they can't make more a mess of it than the old country . . . *(Enter MR DIMITRY.)* Come in . . . Don't mind me I'm talking to myself . . . You get that way when you spend a lot of time on the veld . . .

MR DIMITRY *(has his hands clasped together).* Mrs Dimitry is having a lie down after dinner . . . *(Pauses.)* Any of us could be taken at any time . . . I've seen so much of it . . . When I close the door on my beloved I wonder if I'll see her in the flesh again . . . Why, sir, any of us may drop dead any moment . . . I've seen so much of it . . . Thrombosis, sir . . . May I have a little of that whisky mixed with a lot of water . . . I told Doris I was going to — I'm too old to go behind her back . . .

There is a tray of drinks on a table. BILL *is fixing his drink. He does one for* MR DIMITRY.

BILL. How can you tell a heart attack?

MR DIMITRY. How can *I* tell a heart attack? Well I could tell if you had one 'cos you'd drop on the floor in front of me . . .

BILL. And then I suppose you'd measure me up?

MR DIMITRY. Well I can take a joke . . . we get a lot of jokes . . . But you would look beautiful laid out . . . I can tell those that would . . . *(Laughs — silvery.)* That's a joke . . . we're expected to joke . . . Oh my goodness . . . *(Starts to measure him up — with his hands.)* Do you think we'd have a sense of humour . . . You should come to our morticians annual conference . . . Five dropped dead last year . . . Well it's because we last so long really . . . Felled like an elm . . .

BILL. Who?

MR DIMITRY. The President . . . I must go back and see if she's sleeping . . . You see at our age either of us could be taken at any time . . . Might only be a headache but it could carry her off . . .

MRS DIMITRY *(appears in doorway in nightdress).* Wilmer are you alright?

MR DIMITRY. Yes darling . . .

MRS DIMITRY. Thank God . . . *(She exits.)*

MR DIMITRY. Oh, she's looking fine . . . Thank God — thank God . . . I dread one of us being left alone.

He wanders off to the platform. Stares out at blackness. Mr and MRS LANGTON *come in. They are dressed as before, except she has a shawl now.* ROBERT *always wears a Beatle-type black polo-neck sweater and nondescript trousers, whatever the weather, or country.*

ROBERT. I felt like killing myself when I came to a halt this time . . .

LILLY. We all do . . .

ROBERT. But to feel so useless . . . I mean this is what I've given my life to . . . writing . . . To find it out here — in the middle of Africa . . . I'm no good . . .

LILLY. Every writer thinks that . . .

ROBERT. After twelve years?

LILLY.   You've written two crime books . . .

ROBERT.   You know they were dreadful . . . You told me . . .

LILLY.   What's it matter what I tell you . . . *(Touch of irritation.)* I told you
they were wonderful as well . . .

ROBERT.   Well what do you really think of them?

LILLY.   You never believe me . . . Pour me a drink . . .

ROBERT *(fixes them drinks)*.   I suppose it will hit me later . . . The fact that
I'm never going to write again . . .

LILLY.   Don't worry . . . *(Enter* MR and MRS FLANAGAN.)

FLANAGAN.   Come on Tessa have a drink . . . Don't be so bloody miserable
. . .

TESSA.   You are going to kill me this trip . . .

FLANAGAN.   That's right . . .

TESSA.   I've got a lot of witnesses . . . I'm telling them . . . Give me a gin and
tonic . . .

ROBERT.   I'll do it . . .

FLANAGAN *(letting* ROBERT *do their drinks)*.   Oh she doesn't think I'm
going to poison her . . .

TESSA.   It's got to look like an accident . . . Like happened to Molly . . .

FLANAGAN *(quietly)*.   If I kill you, woman, I want the credit for it . . .
(Generally.) This is her latest line of chat . . . She's got fed up of accusing me
of infidelities . . .

TESSA.   God get me out of Africa and home to mother . . .

She drinks quickly after those words. Door opens and young PIKE *staggers in —
covered in blood.*

BILL.   My God! It's Pike . . .

PIKE.   They got Mary . . . *(They help him.)*

LILLY.   Oh Crikey . . .

ROBERT.   Let me help . . . I'm good at first aid . . . Sit down Pike . . .

PIKE.   What?

BILL.   Get him a whisky . . .

FLANAGAN.   Make that two . . . What's wrong with him?

PIKE.   Tigers . . .

BILL.   Tigers?

MR DIMITRY.   Really? Tigers? I must tell Doris . . . Tigers . . . Tigers . . .
Really tigers? . . . Really tigers . . . That's dreadful . . . Well it said so on the
brochure . . . We should be surprised? I think not . . . The poor chap . . .
Really tigers . . . *(As he goes out)* Doris . . . Really tigers . . .

ROBERT.   He's a mess . . . but he'll be alright . . . *(*BILL *rings bell.*
UMBOKO *appears in doorway.)*

BILL.   Get some water and bandages Umboko! *(As he goes, calls him back)*
Do you know about tigers round here? *(*UMBOKO *stares at him.)* Never
mind Umboko . . . Get the water . . . *(Takes out his list, tries to rub out where
he has crossed out. To* PIKE.*)* How did you get out here you blithering idiot?

PIKE.   Bicycles . . . It's only thirty miles . . . We thought we could make it
before dark . . . Mary's gone . . . I can't believe it . . . It was tigers! *(*BILL *takes
a rifle from the wall, goes to safe and opens it. Takes out cartridges. Loads
gun.)*

BILL.   There haven't been any tigers in these parts for two years . . . There haven't been any bicycles that I know of . . . How did you get hold of bicycles?

PIKE.   Raleigh . . .

BILL.   I don't care about the make . . .

PIKE.   Mary . . .

BILL.   How far?

PIKE.   Two miles from the water hole . . . We could see the lights of the hide . . .

FRED *and* EMMA *enter.* FRED *in suave dinner jacket,* EMMA *wears dark suit.*

FRED.   What's happened to him? Go and ask . . .

EMMA.   He's hurt . . .

FRED.   Go and ask what it is . . . Then come and tell me . . .

EMMA.   Looks like he's been scratched with some forks . . .

FRED.   Just ask what's happened . . . I can't bear accidents . . . I don't want to look . . . I'm pleading with you . . . get me the information . . . *(*EMMA *goes to the group round* PIKE.*)*

EMMA.   What's the matter with him?

ROBERT.   Tigers . . . *(*EMMA *goes back to* FRED.*)*

EMMA.   Tigers . . .

FRED.   Tigers? You said forks . . . Are you sure you asked properly . . .

EMMA.   Forks is what it looks like . . . As though he's been scratched with forks . . .

FRED.   I'm not interested in appearances . . . least of all yours tonight . . . Go and ask if we can help . . .

EMMA.   Help? How can we help? *(*UMBOKO *has brought hot water and first aid things.)*

BILL *(to* UMBOKO*).*   Get your spear Umboko . . . We're going after tigers . . . Get Subaba . . . Quick . . .

UMBOKO.   He's doing the washin' up . . .

BILL.   I said tigers . . .

UMBOKO.   He can't be in two places at the same time . . . If he's doing the washing up he can't do tigers . . . make up your mind . . .

BILL.   Tigers come first damn it!

UMBOKO.   You won't get your breakfast in the morning . . . not if your plates aren't washed . . . make up your mind . . . what do you want — hotel service?

BILL.   Alright Umboko . . . Just you and I will go . . .

UMBOKO.   OK . . . I'll fetch my spear . . . *(Pauses at door.)* I'm on overtime after nine o'clock you know that?

BILL.   Yes . . . *(*UMBOKO *exits.* FLANAGAN *takes other gun from wall.)*

FLANAGAN.   I'm coming. I'm a good shot . . .

TESSA.   You're not going darling! You're not going anywhere.

FLANAGAN.   Darling? So the trip to Africa is having effect . . . It is saving our marriage . . . primitive times . . . primitive emotions . . .

TESSA.   Don't go out there! It's so black! You might get hurt . . .

FLANAGAN.   Will you tell these people you were blackening my name? I'm trying to kill you . . .

TESSA. No you're not . . .

FLANAGAN. I killed my first wife?

TESSA. No . . . that was a car accident . . .

FLANAGAN. You're taking too many pills Tessa . . . You're frightened of
growing old . . . So you're taking pills . . . At twenty-three you're frightened
that you're finished? Why don't you start to live? *(UMBOKO joins them
with his spear.)*

BILL. Come on . . . *(To* PIKE.*)* Were you on the track?

PIKE. Yes . . . By the trees . . .

BILL. That's only a mile . . . Come on . . . *(To* PIKE.*)* Bicycles! Where did
you get bicycles?

PIKE. All the Africans are riding them . . .

BILL. I hadn't noticed . . . I thought they were walking . . .

UMBOKO. You go round with your head in the sand . . . Don't you hear
about Macmillan's wind of change? We're all riding bicycles now . . . Ain't
you seen my cousin? The one with the clips round his ears? The bicycle clips?

BILL. I never know when you're kidding, Umboko . . .

BILL, UMBOKO *and* FLANAGAN *exit.*

ACT TWO

Scene 1

*The next morning. Just before dawn. The light is already filtering in through the
observation window, and the birds are beginning to sing.*
Onstage are BILL *and* PIKE. BILL *gives* PIKE *bundle of notes.*

BILL. There you are . . . fifty pounds . . . that's the arrangement . . .

PIKE. That's not much . . .

BILL. What do you mean that's not much . . . that's what we arranged isn't it?

PIKE. There's the girl . . .

BILL. I didn't ask your wretched girl friend to get eaten by a tiger, did I . . . if
you want to row her in that's your business . . . comes out of your cut . . .

PIKE. Only . . . she'll blab unless I giver her some money . . .

BILL. I didn't want her eaten by the tigers . . . you know that . . . It's going too
far . . .

PIKE. She wasn't eaten. She escaped you see. Unharmed. and ran back to the
mission station . . . The tigers were concentrating on me . . . I wasn't to
know . . .

BILL. It's too complicated . . . You shouldn't have brought her into the story
in the first place . . . It's you I wanted eaten by the tigers . . . Nobody else . . .

PIKE. Those scratches cost me a lot of . . .

BILL. What?

PIKE. Blood . . . I threw myself into a thorn . . . thicket . . . getting out was
hell.

BILL. Well why drag the girl into it . . .

PIKE. I didn't drag her into the thicket . . . Look here it was your idea to get publicity for your clapped out firm ... Tigers? Nobody's seen tigers for years ...

BILL.   They're still around ...

PIKE.   The point is chum ... You was going bust without the wild animals to sustain you ... Now you want a bit of publicity ... for your tours ... your safaris ...

BILL.   I should never have bought this business you know ... When the other chap sold out he knew what he was doing ...

PIKE.   Well a bit of blood and thunder and danger will put a bit of spice back into your publicity ... You should have them flocking along now ... Now I want another twenty pounds ... I've got to face the press, haven't I ... I've got to make it look like my carelessness — not a badly run tour op ...

BILL.   I'll say not ... safety first ...

PIKE.   You want the best of both worlds.

BILL.   Well you can't have safety first unless you've got some fall back into danger that you're protecting them from ... It's a wild scheme — I wish I'd never done it ... It was the whisky ... *(BILL pays him more money.)* Twenty ...

PIKE.   That'll keep the girl quiet ...

BILL.   You're a bounder Pike ... Don't come back to me for more money ...

PIKE.   No fear ... I still say homo sapiens is the most dangerous ... I won't push you too far ... *(He goes to door.)* I'll be off then ... Shall I take the truck?

BILL.   Go with Subaba ... He can drive the truck back ... Pike ...

PIKE.   Yes?

BILL.   I'm warning you, Pike, you better make the story stick ...

PIKE.   Oh yes ... Don't want to cross the path of the White Hunter do we ... Ha! *(He leaves.)*

BILL.   Where are those boys? They should have woken the others by now ... They'll miss it again ... They'll miss the blasted wild life ... *(Looks out of window.)* Ohh there's a few giraffe there today ... *(He exits calling.)* Boy! Umboko! Umboko, you Ace of Spades you!

Enter MR DIMITRY *in dressing-gown and* FRED *in pyjamas.*

MR DIMITRY.   Good morning ... shouldn't everybody be up? I'm sure something's going to happen ... I heard the birds calling ... I went into Doris ... She's still with us ...

FRED.   Pardon?

MR DIMITRY.   How many cases do I know of a loved one who's gone in the night in their sleep ...

FRED.   Gone? Where? Oh I see ...

MR DIMITRY.   It's sad ... but it's not that bad ... They can look beautiful ... She's still breathing thank God ... Another day ... Sometimes I wake up and she's looking at me ... and I say to her 'I'm still here' ... Well we live our life a day at a time don't we ... ?

FRED *(seems rather worried)*.   Yep ... *(Pauses.)* Why? Why does that boy sleep with a knife in his hand?

MR DIMITRY.   Pardon?

FRED.   That boy ... Michael ... That is my private secretary ... He

can't sleep without a knife in his hand . . . he can't sleep . . . Isn't that odd? An
odd habit wouldn't you say?

MR DIMITRY.   Oh it takes all sorts to make a world . . . I've seen some
strange things in my sleep . . .

Enter MRS DIMITRY *in dressing-gown — rather baby-doll frilly thing.*

MRS DIMITRY.   Mr Dimitry . . .

MR DIMITRY.   Yes my love . . .

MRS DIMITRY.   I looked in your bunk . . .

MR DIMITRY.   And I was risen . . . Never mind — I should have left a note
. . . That would have been ridiculous . . .

MRS DIMITRY.   Fetch the cameras . . .

MR DIMITRY.   Yes my angel . . . *(He exits.)*

MRS DIMITRY *(at the window)*.   Ohh there's a nice lot animals there . . .
They're all gathering at the water . . . Isn't it a beautiful sight?

FRED *(who doesn't bother to look)*.   Yes . . . (BILL *enters.)*

BILL.   Have you seen Umboko?

FRED.   No.

BILL.   Good morning . . . Didn't he bring you tea?

FRED.   I believe not . . .

BILL.   Blast . . . *(He goes through the door to the sleeping quarters. As he
goes)* Come along everybody! Let's be having you! Hands off your socks
and. . . ! Oh never mind that . . . Please hurry everybody! Or you'll miss
everything *(He is off — talking.)* No there's no tea this morning . . . I'm
frightfully sorry . . .

Enter MR DIMITRY *with two cameras. Gives one to his wife.*

MRS DIMITRY.   What kept you?

MR DIMITRY.   That's a good one . . .   *(To* FRED.*)* Haven't you got a
camera?

FRED.   I suppose I'd — I'd better . . .

MR DIMITRY *(taking* FRED *aside)*.   My friend, if it makes you feel any
better . . . I've got a son who sleeps with a revolver under his pillow . . . At
least he did do . . .

FRED.   How — how did he stop the habit?

MR DIMITRY.   Well he shot three policemen and . . . what? In the
penitentiary he doesn't sleep with a revolver in under his pillow . . . Now he
was a well brought up boy I won't have it any different . . .

FRED.   Thank you . . .

MR DIMITRY *(still detaining him)*.   He found God in jail you know . . . So
the Lord works in mysterious ways . . .

FRED.   I must get my camera . . .

MR DIMITRY.   Now that's called sharing my friend . . . *(*FRED *stares at* MR
DIMITRY, *not knowing how to answer.)*

FRED.   It's — it's just . . . Thank you . . . *(He exits.)*

MR *and* MRS LANGTON *enter — nightwear — and cameras.*

LILLY.   How do you work this thing?

ROBERT.   And you a journalist . . .

LILLY.   Not a photographer . . .

ROBERT.   Here . . . *(He shows her how to work the camera.)*

Enter FLANAGAN *—in an extraordinary nightshirt.*

FLANAGAN *(displaying nightshirt)*.   Do you like it. . . ? (LILLY *gives a little clap.)* I won it . . . It was one of the spoils of a film I was in . . . Guess?

LILLY.   Errm . . . *Wuthering Heights?*

FLANAGAN.   No . . .

LILLY.   I give up . . .

FLANAGAN.   Well it was *David Copperfield* . . .

LILLY.   And it still fits you . . . What a surprise . . .

FLANAGAN.   I played the older David Copperfield . . .

LILLY.   It would appear so . . . Excuse me . . .

FLANAGAN.   Get her . . . I'm wasting my time here . . .   *(Enter his wife.)* What is this? A pyjama party?

TESSA *(sleepy)*.   Have you got the camera? I forgot mine . . .

FLANAGAN.   When I see you like this in the morning . . . so cuddly . . . I'm reminded . . . Of the time I came home early off that film in Ireland and found you in the arms of my best mate . . . As he then was . . .

TESSA.   What were you doing? What were you doing in Ireland? And what were you doing in Mexico? And Iceland? It's you that liberated me . . . You told me to get on with my own life and stop moaning . . .

FLANAGAN.   I'm not complaining . . . It hurts that's all . . . *(*BILL *enters.)*

BILL.   No flash! Now no flash ladies and gentlemen or they'll hoof it! Softee softee catchee monkey! Now all on the platform please! Let's have lots of 'ush shall we!

They gather on the platform. FRED *enters pushing or pulling* EMMA *— who is still in last night's clothes he has been sleeping in.* EMMA *obstinately drops into a chair.*

FRED.   I'm pleading with you! This is the big one Michael! Please take some photos for me . . .   *(There are cries and exclamations — muted — from the window.)*

MRS DIMITRY.   Isn't that a zebra? That one with stripes on?

FLANAGAN.   I believe it is . . . How clever of you . . . The vanishing wilderness . . . Isn't that a cow?

MRS DIMITRY.   They don't have cows here . . .

FLANAGAN.   They do . . .

ROBERT *(to* LILLY *as they take photos)*.   This is what we came for . . .

LILLY.   I'm glad you think so . . .

ROBERT.   Isn't it? I don't have to be a writer do I? I can be a human being . . . Well?

LILLY.   Stop torturing yourself . . . I don't mind . . .

ROBERT.   It's just that I'm happy this morning . . .

LILLY.   Well don't keep talking about it . . .

BILL.   With any luck we'll see the rhinos . . . No not this morning . . .

FRED *(to* EMMA *still in chair)*.   Please . . .

EMMA.   Take your own bloody pictures . . .

FRED. I hired you as my private secretary . . .

EMMA. I do enough for you . . .

FRED. What?

EMMA. You've got a bum boy . . .

FRED. That's a — an awful thing to say . . . We're friends — we're not responsible for that . . .

EMMA. Get lost . . .

FRED. Very well . . . I'll take the pictures . . . And I'll let you have copies . . . And if you want to tread all over me you shall . . . Because I love you . . .

EMMA. I took pictures in the flat . . .

FRED. Oh . . . *(Surprised.)*

EMMA. Of the wild life . . . I'll let you have copies . . . at a price . . . I'll let you have the originals . . . at a price . . .

FRED. I don't believe you . . . You wouldn't do such a thing . . .

EMMA. We've all got a living to make . . . You and your wife have made yours in property . . . I make mine in 'views' . . . *(FRED slumps down into another chair.)*

MRS DIMITRY. Isn't that a pair of kangaroos?

MR DIMITRY. No dear . . . you only get them in Australia . . .

MRS DIMITRY. Where are we? Oh of course Africa . . . Are we going to Australia?

MR DIMITRY. No it's not on the itinerary . . .

MRS DIMITRY *(aggressively)*. Well what are they?

MR DIMITRY. They're those animals that put their heads in the sand . . . Ostriches . . .

MRS DIMITRY. Why do they put their heads in the sand?

MR DIMITRY. I don't know . . .

FLANAGAN. Because they're married . . . and they can't bear the sight of each other . . .

There is a shot — off. Quite loud. The bird noises come up . . . and disappear.

BILL. Blast! Who fired that . . . ?

MRS DIMITRY. What were they shooting at? The animals have gone . . . Wilmer — did you get everything?

MR DIMITRY. I'll say I did . . . everything on hoof . . .

MRS DIMITRY. What about the birds?

MR DIMITRY. I didn't get the birds . . . suddenly it's birds . . . I didn't know you were interested in birds Doris . . .

BILL. Calm down everybody . . .

FLANAGAN. We are quite calm . . . Mr Bill . . . I suggest you follow our example . . .

BILL. What?

FLANAGAN. Was that supposed to happen that shot? Was that the grand finale?

BILL. Never . . . Please excuse me . . .

ROBERT. That's funny . . . I didn't see any animal fall . . .

LILLY. The shot was probably to frighten them . . .

ROBERT. Away? Who'd do that?

LILLY.   Well you're the one who's always coming up with thrillers . . . Can't you find a motive? *(BILL has gone to the door.)*

BILL.   I'm very sorry ladies and gentlemen . . . there must have been an accidental firing . . . But the animals would not have stayed much longer I can assure you . . .   *(As he turns to go PIKE enters.)*

PIKE.   The transport's gone . . .

BILL.   Oh . . .

PIKE.   No sign of the boys . . . What's up?

BILL.   Did you fire that shot?

PIKE.   Course I didn't . . . Do you think I'm barmy . . .

BILL.   Then who did? Who the hell did? I'm in enough trouble . . . I never should have bought this racket you know . . . Come on . . .   *(BILL and PIKE exit.)*

FLANAGAN.   Anyone for tennis? What time's breakfast? Are you enjoying the trip, madam? *(Suddenly grabs his wife.)* Put some clothes on . . .

TESSA.   Why?

FLANAGAN.   Because I can't bear it that's why . . . Did you have to sleep with him?

TESSA.   No . . .

FLANAGAN.   Then why . . .

TESSA.   Because I read it's good for the figure . . .

FLANAGAN.   What?

TESSA.   Regular sex . . . And you were away . . . I told you not to do that picture . . .

FLANAGAN.   You had sex with my mate cos it's good for your figure? Where did you read that?

TESSA.   I thought you'd lost interest . . .

FLANAGAN.   Did you tell him? Did you tell the poor bugger you were just doing it because of your hips . . . ? Get out . . .   *(This has been a scarce concealed row. TESSA runs out in tears. FLANAGAN turns round and finds ROBERT.)* She did it for the good of her figure . . .

ROBERT.   Oh . . .

FLANAGAN.   Now that's going to look good in a divorce court isn't it? Since I started going with my husband's friends I have lost six inches round my waist . . . And gained it *(Breaks off sentence)* . . . Dahhh . . . It's my fault . . . You see I'm promiscuous . . . That's what equality of the sexes gives you . . .

ROBERT.   I'd like you to read one of my books one day . . . If you've time . . . Well it might make a good film . . . It's a sort of cheap . . . perhaps not . . . no the payoff's lame . . . still it could be rewritten . . . perhaps not . . .   *(He looks disappointed.)*

FLANAGAN.   Do you usually talk your way out of big deals . . .

ROBERT.   It's about archaeology . . . a trip . . . I can see I'm losing your attention . . .

FLANAGAN.   You never had it . . . I shouldn't worry about it . . . *(Abstracted.)* That bitch . . .

LILLY *(pats settee where she is sitting).*   Do sit down Mr Flanagan . . . You look upset . . . Didn't you get the pictures you wanted?

FLANAGAN *(sits beside her).*   What?

LILLY.   Of the animals? The wild life?

124 *John Antrobus*

FLANAGAN. Oh ... No ... What are you talking to me for?
LILLY (*confiding*). I find my husband rather boring ... (*adds to soften it.*)
    At the moment ...
FLANAGAN. That makes two of us ... Would you lift your legs up?
LILLY. What?
FLANAGAN. For me? Forgive me ... it's the wild life ... it's being out here
    ... it's making me crude and vulgar ... It's the longing for excitement ... We
    were promised it ...
LILLY. What about the tigers?
FLANAGAN. So you're still talking to me ... ?
LILLY. I'm happily married ... Well I'm married ... (*She touches*
    FLANAGAN's *hand.*) That is ... I've never been unfaithful ...
FLANAGAN. It's the heat ... Does things to a woman ... Ha ... I say I'm
    sorry about that legs business ... I'm usually a charmer ...
LILLY. Yes I would ...
FLANAGAN. What?
LILLY. Lift them for you ...
FLANAGAN. Right ...

Scene 2

Later that morning. Only FRED *is onstage. He has not dressed yet. Looks
rather preoccupied.* PIKE *enters and sits on the edge of a chair — nervously.*
FRED *becomes aware of him.*

FRED. How ...
PIKE. Mmmm?
FRED. How ... ?
PIKE. How?
FRED. How are you? How are you? How are you? (*Sometimes* FRED *has
    trouble getting the words out. Then, when he does, they may come out
    quickly.*)
PIKE. Fine ...
FRED. Are you recovered? From your mauling? Are you?
PIKE. Oh yes ...
FRED. Good ... I beg of you ...
PIKE. What?
FRED. Don't ... tell Emma ...
PIKE. Tell Emma ... ?
FRED. That is Michael ... don't tell Michael ... that we've spoken — he gets
    so jealous ... Are you recovered in spirits?
PIKE. Oh yes ...
FRED. After your wife has been eaten by a tiger? That's remarkable ... Mind
    you — you were honeymooners ... that ... must make some difference ...
    Well if err ... you'd known her years you would never never never ...
PIKE. Eh?
FRED. Recover so quickly ... In fact if she were going to be eaten by a tiger
    the sooner the better for your sake emotionally ...

PIKE. Quite . . . well she wasn't eaten . . .

FRED. Oh . . .

PIKE. No, remarkable occurrence she made it back to the mission station unharmed . . .

FRED. That is remarkable . . .

PIKE. That is remarkable . . . They cabled through . . . wireless . . . Yes . . .

FRED. I see . . . congratulations . . . I should imagine that you're very proud . . . to have chased the tiger off her . . . to have attracted it to yourself . . . Never mind . . .

PIKE. You see . . . I was going back this morning . . . but there's no natives about . . . I mean they've nicked the transport or something . . . gone to a union meeting . . .

FRED. Ohhh . . .

PIKE. What?

FRED. Ohhh . . .

PIKE. Yes . . . *(He is rather rough in speech.)* See today or tomorrow is it . . . Well they're hanging seven blacks . . . seven Africans . . . anti-terrorist laws . . . It's made them unsettled.

FRED. It would me if I was being hung . . . I didn't imagine you'd get so much of it down this part of the country . . . I mean I'd heard . . .

PIKE. What?

FRED. Heard . . . Of them . . . But I didn't expect that the hangings would upset the natives down this far . . . That's very good news about your wife . . . Well I expect you think so . . .

PIKE. I do . . . I do . . .

FRED. You don't have to convince me . . . marriage is good for most people . . . I'm married . . . I still have to take business trips . . . *(Before PIKE can ask.)* Is this a business trip? Yes . . . I've heard there's oil round these parts do you know anything about it?

PIKE. Not me mate. *(He stands.)*

FRED. You're very attractive — she's very lucky . . . Can you type? Take shorthand? Doesn't matter . . . Only I'm looking for an able entrepreneur type of chap. Do anything type of fellow . . . money's good . . . when your honeymoon's finished . . . *(Fishes card out of his dressing gown. Gives it to PIKE.)* Phone me . . .

PIKE. Ta mate . . . might look you up . . .

FRED. I hope you do . . . I shall have a staff shortage very soon . . . You don't sleep with a knife do you? '

MICHAEL *enters. He is casually dressed with a clean shirt on, which is beautiful. He stares at PIKE. PIKE exits.*

MICHAEL. Paying me off are you? You'll only get into trouble with new staff . . .

FRED. I'm always having trouble with my staff . . . *(Enter BILL.)*

BILL. I'm sorry about the delay . . . I was going to move you out at noon . . . Well you've had a good sighting haven't you . . . And the weather doesn't look too good.

FRED. I thought we stayed here two nights . . . ?

BILL. Yes . . .

FRED.   Well stick to that story chum . . . You want to move us out because the natives are in an ugly mood is that it?

BILL.   I don't want it to get to the ladies . . .

FRED.   Yes I know all that . . . But someone's whipped the transport . . . So if you don't make a fuss who's going to know the difference . . . Are you in the red? Is this your firm is it? Not the best scotch . . .

BILL.   In the best bottles . . .

FRED.   I've seen that little rat Pike in one of those bars in Salisbury . . . I've seen him down as far as Nairobi . . . What's he doing on a honeymoon trip with you Bill? I can buy you out lock stock and barrel . . .

BILL.   Wish you would . . .

FRED.   Any land go with this hut?

BILL.   'Bout thirty acres . . .

FRED.   I buy up bits of nowhere you know that? And bits of nobody . . . on a hunch . . . I could buy you . . .

BILL.   Well I'm going very cheap at the moment . . .

FRED.   I know you are . . . I can sense it . . . Michael make a note . . . Big Bill Safari Enterprises . . . thirty acres . . . *(MICHAEL takes out notebook with a tuck-in silver pencil. Takes note.)* And the base camp?

BILL.   That's all mortgaged . . .

FRED.   And so is this . . . No — you can't mortgage the wilderness . . . Well it will all be dust and ashes one day . . .

BILL.   Don't let on that Pike's a local character . . .

FRED.   Of unsavoury reputation . . .

MICHAEL.   What?

FRED.   Not for your ears . . . *(BILL exits.)*

MICHAEL.   You think you can buy anybody don't you?

FRED.   Yes . . . Of a certain type . . .

MICHAEL.   You won't buy Bill's bum — it's fireproof . . .

FRED.   He's one of the Few you know . . .

MICHAEL.   Few what?

FRED.   Well a bomber pilot . . . a man's man . . . We're in trouble out here Michael my boy . . . You wanted to get away from it all didn't you? One of your other clients you'd been blackmailing no doubt . . . turned on you . . .

MICHAEL.   I don't do it for the money I do it for the excitement . . . I worked in an office block in Salisbury for three years playing little poufs at the weekend . . . but I was selling myself short . . . so I got out while I was still young . . .

FRED.   Of prostitution?

MICHAEL.   No office work . . . It's degrading . . . It uses none of my talents . . . Why are you planning to buy up thirty acres of nothing . . . There's nothing here . . . ?

FRED.   I'm a fairy godmother . . . I strike where I like . . . where I like . . . Did you see the animals round that waterhole? It was pathetic . . . looked like a lot of unemployed actors in skins to me . . .

MICHAEL.   The wilderness is receding . . .

FRED.   Yes fortunately you're replacing it with a wilderness of your own . . . Let me come to you . . . I only want to lie beside you . . .

MICHAEL.   The only fun I get out of this is tormenting you . . . That's my
      game . . . Fairy godmother . . .
FRED.   Did you take snapshots that weekend at the flat?
MICHAEL.   You were too drunk to know . . .
FRED.   Why do you do it?
MICHAEL.   To reduce your power . . .
FRED.   I cringe to you already . . . what more do you want?
MICHAEL.   A lot of your money . . . Then I'm going to get out of this racket
      and get married . . . I'm going to find a nice girl and get married . . .
FRED.   Oh . . . You're pathetic . . .
MICHAEL (*nearly in tears*).   I'm glad you think so . . .
FRED.   You'll never get out of whoring you won't . . . the money's too easy . . .
      Blackmail? You couldn't blackmail me . . . I'd have you done over . . . That's
      why you're on the run already . . . into my arms . . . my protection . . .
MICHAEL.   Damn you. (*Very upset.*) Alright . . . there aren't any snap-
      shots . . .
FRED.   Now will you let me help you?
MICHAEL.   Yes.
FRED.   You try to intimidate me? Oh you are a big bully . . . You want to
      marry one day? Only I can help you to do that . . . Let me come to you . . . Let
      me love you . . .
MICHAEL.   I want . . . girls . . . a girl . . . I don't know . . .
FRED.   I'll find you a girl you silly boy. I can find you the only girl in your life
      . . . I can find you anything you want . . . Only let me love you . . . It will help
      you on your way to a good marriage I promise you . . . I didn't know you
      wanted to get married . . . You should have told me. Do you think I would
      leave you stranded . . . Of course you'll marry. If you'll just trust me . . . I
      won't harm you . . .
MICHAEL.   Will there ever be a girl . . . ?
FRED.   At the end of your rainbow sonny . . . ? Oh yes . . . yes . . . *(*FRED
      cuddles him.)* I'm married . . . Come and help me get dressed . . .
MICHAEL.   In a minute . . .

FRED *exits.* MICHAEL *sits in a chair, facing downstage, trying to get it
together. Enter* UMBOKO *in a fierce tiger mask. They don't see each other.*
UMBOKO *looks round. Finds camera, which apparently is what he is looking
for. Exits.* MICHAEL *stands and goes to the door as* MR *and* MRS DIMITRY
enter.

MR DIMITRY (*taking* MICHAEL *by the arm*).   Why, young man I've got a
      little daughter who would suit you down to the ground . . . only divorced
      once . . . *(To his wife.)* Margaret . . . wouldn't Margaret suit this young man?
MRS DIMITRY.   Oh he doesn't want a has-been woman . . . he wants a
      virgin. . .
MICHAEL.   Well . . .
MR DIMITRY.   Are we embarrassing you?
MICHAEL.   No.
MR DIMITRY.   Our daughter made a mistake the first time. No kiddies thank
      God . . . she can start afresh . . . Are you fixed up? Are you engaged young
      man?

MICHAEL. No . . .

MR DIMITRY. Look us up. Well I say it Mother . . . I know it's not likely . . .
(To MICHAEL.*)* But it's not often you meet such a well presented young
man . . .

MICHAEL. You don't know much about me sir . . .

MR DIMITRY. Don't want to . . . should I? If you want to confess anything to
me that doesn't make you a worse man than I am . . . Why my own son . . .

MRS DIMITRY. Wilmer . . .

MR DIMITRY. Let me tell him Mother . . .

MRS DIMITRY. You're telling everybody . . . But if you want to Wilmer . . .

MR DIMITRY. Thank you . . . *(To* MICHAEL.*)* My own son is a convicted
murderer . . . Now you look at me and say 'where did he get it' . . . He got it
from a whited sepulchre. 'Come to church' I said to him . . . 'Meet God' but
was God in my heart? No sirree . . . You know who killed those cops? I did.

MRS DIMITRY *(disturbed)*. Dad . . .

MR DIMITRY. Mother let me . . .

MRS DIMITRY. Alright . . .

MR DIMITRY. I killed them . . . the sins of the forefathers are visited upon us
. . . I killed them as if I was standing in front of them . . . and why? Because I
could not show the charity of Christ to my own son . . . Faith . . . Hope . . .
but no charity . . . And the greatest of the three is charity — St Paul said . . . 'If
I speak in the tongues of men and of angels, but have not love, I am a noisy
gong or a clanging cymbal. And if I have prophetic powers and understand
all mysteries, and all knowledge, and if I have all faith, so as to remove
mountains, but have not love, I am nothing. If I give away all I have, and if I
deliver my body to be burned, but have not love, I gain nothing' . . . I killed
those cops *(MRS DIMITRY takes his arm.)*

MRS DIMITRY. There, there Dad . . . Don't pay no heed to him son . . .

MICHAEL. He helped me . . . Thank you . . .

MR DIMITRY. Look us up . . .

MRS DIMITRY. Let's go on the verandah Wilmer . . .

MR DIMITRY. OK . . . *(They exit.)*

MICHAEL. And have not love . . . I am nothing . . . *(He exits — other side.
Enter* BILL *and* PIKE.*)*

BILL *(looks round to make sure none of the guests are about. Points to wall.)*
The guns were put back there . . . They're gone!

PIKE. Never mind that . . .

BILL. I put the shells back in the safe . . .

PIKE. I reckon Fred is sniffing around for a deal . . .

BILL. What would he want with a clapped out old travel firm?

PIKE. Thirty acres . . .

BILL. I know I've had it chum . . . but I'll keep on going . . . *(He goes to the
safe, and opens it to look for shells.)* One more safari . . . There's always the
next trip . . . There's always a few more . . .

PIKE. Why don't you retire?

BILL. To what? Oblivion . . . I've invested money in your bloody wildcap
scheme of publicity . . . That might be a shot in the arm for us for a little
while . . .

PIKE.   I'm your publicity agent . . .

BILL.   No you're not . . . *(No shells in safe.)* They're gone . . . The ammunition has been taken . . . Who could open this safe? Anyone . . . Umboko . . . It's a job to keep the door shut . . . Sometimes it swings open . . . I say to people you can keep your valuables in there . . . something wrong with the lock . . . Still it looks good . . .

PIKE.   Fred will give you a good price . . .

BILL.   Cash would be the ruination of me . . . whisky . . . I'd kill myself with drink . . . You know — there might be geothermal rock under here . . . If you go down far enough . . . couple of miles . . . Well there's geothermal rock under everywhere really if you go down far enough . . . I wonder if that's what the blighter's after . . .

PIKE.   Have you got any hot springs round here . . .

BILL.   No . . . They pump water down to the hot rock and it comes back as steam and energy . . . Think of it . . . I'm standing on a gold mine . . . Everybody is . . . *(Enter FLANAGAN.)*

FLANAGAN *(to* PIKE). You're up and about . . . fully recovered?

PIKE.   Yes thanks . . . scratches . . .

FLANAGAN.   Not going into mourning I hope . . . it won't help . . .

PIKE.   Oh . . . oh yes . . . good news . . . the missus . . . that is the wife like . . . she's alive . . . she escaped unharmed and got to a mission station . . .

FLANAGAN.   You mean the tigers didn't eat her?

PIKE.   No . . .

FLANAGAN.   Hard luck . . . What's this mean — a divorce?

PIKE.   Well we've only just come together . . .

FLANAGAN.   Don't waste any time . . . don't spoil it all with recrimination *(He leaves).*

BILL.   You go and pick up your bike . . . and get to the mission station and get them to radio for transport . . . I want this lot out of here as soon as possible . . .

PIKE.   Feeling uneasy?

BILL.   The boys have taken the guns . . . Now I don't mind if they pop off . . . pop off to their union meetings. But they shouldn't take the arms . . . I mean that is against the spirit of our agreement . . . It's showing off really . . . Now I don't like a native to show off . . .

PIKE.   They're hanging seven of them today . . . down in Salisbury . . .

BILL.   I doubt whether my boys even know about it . . . They're not that way inclined . . . they're jovial types . . . they've seen what ownership does to a man . . . they don't want any of it . . . If they want to run this Big Bill Safari Enterprises then they're welcome to it . . . But they've got no right to take the bloody transport just because they've got some bloody shop-steward calling them to the hills . . . convening a tribal thing . . .

PIKE.   Is my bike up there?

BILL.   Yes, now get going . . .

PIKE.   If I do a deal with Fred for you . . . I'll expect ten percent . . . *(He exits.)*

BILL.   Breakfast . . . Better get them some breakfast . . . *(Has second thoughts.)* Brunch! Better call it brunch . . . Can serve alcohol with it then . . . *(As* BILL *goes to exit to kitchens,* UMBOKO *steps in, wearing tiger-head mask.)* Umboko you rascal! Now what's all this you peeing off to union meetings? Now look I'll have the employers down on you . . . And — and I'm not impressed with that costume . . . Masonic afair if I ever saw one . . . We did better than that in Croydon . . . (UMBOKO *takes off the mask. Stands impassively in front of* BILL.) Well have you got the breakfast ready? If you want a rise why don't you ask for one? I suggest workers shares . . . Speak to Subaba about it . . . Now come let's have some breakfast . . . Umboko . . . We've known each other too long . . . what's the matter? Who's been getting at you?

UMBOKO.   Seven terrorists die today boss . . .

BILL.   Yes well that's nothing to do with me . . . I've had my war . . . I suppose Dresden was nothing to do with some of them either . . . Well if you want to roast us on toast get on with it . . . I could have incorporated you lot in a publicity scheme . . . An element of danger, we could have worked out something good . . . How about it? Haven't been drinking the whisky? No . . .

UMBOKO.   Seven black terrorists die today in Salisbury boss . . .

BILL.   Yes I know, yes . . . well I can't do anything about it . . . If you want to take over that's up to you . . . I'll work for you . . . I'll work for anyone . . . Do you want to buy me out, you and your chums . . . All I want's enough for the occasional binge-up . . . If you've got pals who can put some money into this firm . . . Just get me on the payroll I'm quite happy . . . No? What is it Umboko?

UMBOKO.   You is under arrest?

BILL.   Who . . . who's arresting us?

UMBOKO.   The liberation army . . .

BILL.   They're not down this far don't be so stupid . . .

UMBOKO.   We are down this far . . .

BILL.   No you're not . . .

UMBOKO.   I'm standing here to tell you that we are down this far . . .

BILL.   Well I'm telling you . . . *(FLANAGAN runs in.)*

FLANAGAN.   There's seven of them! They've just strung up Pike! *(UMBOKO puts his mask back on* MR *and* MRS DIMITRY *come in.)*

MRS DIMITRY.   This will be the end of us . . . It's worse than Detroit.

MR DIMITRY.   They don't look such bad fellows . . . *(FLANAGAN runs back to door.)*

FLANAGAN.   He's swinging there! They're taking photographs of him . . . *(MRS DIMITRY sees* UMBOKO *in his mask.)*

MRS DIMITRY.   Ohhh! Quick Wilmer! Get him . . .

MR DIMITRY.   Right . . .

MR DIMITRY *quickly takes out light meter. Holds it against* UMBOKO *Loads flash. Takes photos. After allowing this, and a few poses* UMBOKO *exits.* FRED *enters. Senses something is wrong and crosses to other door.*

FRED.   My God . . . They got Pike . . . Bill you'd better get on your radio . . .

BILL.   I can't . . . the battery's clapped out . . .

FRED.   You're under-capitalised you know that . . . *(MICHAEL enters.)*

MICHAEL.   What's wrong?

FRED.   No don't look . . .

MICHAEL.   Why not?

FRED.   I'm pleading with you . . .   *(He tries to hold* MICHAEL *back.* MICHAEL *pushes him away and goes to door. Calmly surveys the scene.)* Come away . . .

MICHAEL *(quite coolly).*   What's this mean?

FLANAGAN.   It means we're some sort of hostages, man . . .

FRED.   Not quite, it doesn't . . . You see the Massowi faction . . . they're the ones that have been arrested . . . they're to be hung . . . Well the Nibos were up in arms against them . . . because they're much more left wing . . . Look, it's all too complicated . . . It means that this lot basically want those seven hung . . . so that they can assume the leadership . . . see? Do you see? Mind you, they must protest and give them the mantle — the crown of martyrdom . . . But we — the whites — are doing their dirty work for them . . . It's very Macbeth — I thoroughly recommend it . . .   *(Repeats.)* I thoroughly recommend it . . . for back-stabbing they're streets ahead of us you know . . . they're as sophisticated as anybody . . .

FLANAGAN.   So Pike's been done as a gesture has he? To solidarity?

FRED.   Oh yes . . . Poor Pike . . . Because I move around in circles that make it possible to pick up this information you know . . . I'm surprised that it's spread out here though . . . Michael! Come away will you? I'm on my knees . . . *(which he is not.)*

MICHAEL comes away from the door.

MR DIMITRY.   Well if we're not hostages . . . I understand hostages . . . if we're not hostages what are we?

FRED.   Reprisals . . .

MR DIMITRY.   We'd be better off to be hostages . . . then you can negotiate . . .

MRS DIMITRY.   What's that?

MR DIMITRY.   Nothing honey . . .

MRS DIMITRY.   Don't give me that nothing . . . One day we're going to go and you know it as well as I do . . . It will be Today . . . sometime it will be Today that it happens . . . sometime it will be Now . . . We've always known it . . . Now is going to arrive and that's going to be our date with our Maker . . . It's not going to happen Tomorrow it's going to happen Now . . .

MR DIMITRY.   I don't follow you Doris.

MRS DIMITRY.   The only time anything ever happens is Now . . . so it's got to be Now that something happens . . .

BILL.   Breakfast . . .

MRS DIMITRY.   Everything is happening Now . . .

MR DIMITRY.   You gone Buddhist have you? Why don't you sit down . . . We're going to have some breakfast . . . Now . . .

ACT THREE

Scene 1

Some time later. They are all assembled in the room. And all dressed now. Sandwiches and cocktail titbits are being eaten and drinks are being served. MR *and* MRS DIMITRY *are drinking coffee.*

BILL *finds bell and rings it.* UMBOKO *enters wearing tiger mask, carrying a tray of drinks. Serves the comapny.*

LILLY *(as* UMBOKO *serves her).*   Doesn't he look frightening? Is this all part of the proceedings?

BILL.   Oh yes . . . yes . . . a bit of local colour . . .

LILLY.   But it's awful . . . they hung that man Pike . . .

BILL.   Not my boys . . . The same tribe perhaps . . . but it's not their fault . . .

MR DIMITRY.   We're all tarred by the same brush . . . We all fall short of the glory of God . . . We are saved by Grace alone . . .

MRS DIMITRY (*quite firmly*).   Helleluhiah . . .

UMBOKO.   Helleluhiah . . .

LILLY.   I don't understand it? Why can't we go home if there's something wrong? Are we being held prisoner?

BILL.   No . . . they've borrowed the transport ma'am . . . this is one of their festival days . . .

LILLY.   Do they always hang somebody on a festival day? He was one of our party . . .

BILL.   I see how it looks to you . . . Must do . . . Must look that way . . . *(Takes out pipe.)* Be strange if you saw it any differently . . . Let me put it to you this way . . . Pike has been mucking round with the natives . . . with the native women . . .

TESSA.   I thought he was just married . . .

BILL.   That makes it worse doesn't it . . .

TESSA.   But he's hanging out there from a tree . . .

BILL.   Don't think about it . . . Think about something more pleasant . . .

FLANAGAN.   If you worry it will put crows feet round your eyes.

TESSA (*searching for hand mirror*).   Oh dear . . .

BILL *takes* UMBOKO *aside. Meanwhile* SUBABA *in a horrid tiger mask enters and serves a tray of sandwiches.*

BILL.   Umboko . . . I demand an explanation . . .

UMBOKO (*removes his mask*).   It was hot in there . . .

BILL.   You go off . . . you hide the transport . . . you pinch the guns . . . you top old Pike . . . I'm not holding you personally responsible . . . the security forces will want an answer . . . I can't hide that body from them . . .

TESSA *(about* SUBABA*).*   Tell him not to creep up on me!

SUBABA *speaks in an African dialect.*

FRED.   He says do you want the salmon mayonnaise or the crab?

UMBOKO (*to* BILL).   Pretty soon we got to leave you . . . Join up with the guerilla forces . . .

BILL.   Well I'm very sad to see things take this turn . . . *(*SUBABA *exits.)*

UMBOKO.   Innocent people are going to get hurt . . .

BILL.   That's what I mean . . . It mustn't be allowed . . .

UMBOKO.   You allowed it in Dresden . . .

BILL.   Never mind Dresden . . .

UMBOKO.   We been educated too now boss . . . we know the score . . . Just 'cos we can't drop bombs from a great height man . . . We got to mix with our victims here below . . . It ain't easy . . . If you had to serve cocktails in Dresden before you bombed them . . .

BILL. Alright . . . Never mind Dresden . . . What about Coventry?

UMBOKO. What about Sharpesville man? I'm thinking you're taking this personal and it's not meant that way . . .

BILL. You don't mean us any harm?

UMBOKO. Certainly not . . . But don't come all this innocent lives crap with me . . . You blew that on many raids . . . Bomber Command . . .

BILL. Yes well I know you've made a study of European History . . .

UMBOKO. Don't worry . . . I'm looking after you . . .

SUBABA *enters, with can. Starts pouring petrol in corners, behind furniture etc.*

BILL. What's he doing?

UMBOKO. This place will be going up like a tinder box soon . . . Don't worry — you'll be out of it . . .

UMBOKO *puts on head mask.* BILL *goes up to* SUBABA. BILL *angrily speaks to him in African dialect.* SUBABA *answers in African.* SUBABA *exits.* UMBOKO *follows him.*

BILL. Don't worry everybody . . . We're merely under a form of house arrest until we get our transport back . . . I've had reassurances . . . These aren't bad guys . . . the baddies . . .

LILLY. Have they been pouring petrol around?

TESSA. Ohh we'll all be burnt alive . . .

MRS DIMITRY. Look what happened to Joan of Arc . . .

MR DIMITRY. What did happen to Joan of Arc? Oh yes — she was martyred . . . What a way to arrive in Kingdom Come . . .

MRS DIMITRY. Helleluhiah . . .

FLANAGAN. I wish you wouldn't keep saying that madam . . . *(Jumps up.)* What happens if we break out of here?

BILL. You wouldn't get further than Pike . . .

FLANAGAN. Well if they want six more victims . . . to make seven . . . to make the seven an equivalent of those hanging in Salisbury . . . Put all our names in the hat *(Points at his wife.)* Hers as well . . . You wanted equality? You've got it . . . *(He sits down again. Takes another drink.*

BILL. Ladies and Gentlemen . . . My boys are not used to this sort of behaviour . . . They obviously want things to go on in the same old way . . . Now if we don't alarm them . . . If we don't behave differently . . .

MICHAEL. We'll live?

BILL. Yes . . . But don't give them bad vibrations . . . An animal can sense fear coming off you . . . And it sets them off . . . it's like a trigger . . . So relax everybody . . . enjoy your cocktail hour or brunch or whatever we call it . . . They'll take off soon . . .

FLANAGAN. Who will?

BILL. The Massowi . . . They'll have to take off to the hills now . . . because they've killed God knows how many . . . The point is we don't have to become embroiled in this . . . so just — carry on . . .

FLANAGAN *(to his wife)*.   About that divorce . . . I think it's better we have
    it . . .
TESSA.   Don't leave me . . .
FLANAGAN *(putting his arm round her)*.   It's only danger keeping us
    together . . . We can't live like this all our lives . . .
TESSA.   This can be a lesson to us . . . How much we need each other . . .
FLANAGAN.   Oh Tessa . . . It doesn't operate like that . . . Back in London
    . . . I'm working . . . We're doing the nightclubs . . . You're at the steam baths
    — the masseurs all day . . . That sort of life makes us supine . . .
TESSA.   It doesn't have to . . .
FLANAGAN.   Doesn't it? Will you have a baby if we come out of this?
TESSA.   Yes . . . That'll be more dangerous . . . I know it will . . . for me . . .
FLANAGAN.   How?
TESSA.   Because I had one once . . . It killed him and it nearly killed me . . .
FLANAGAN.   I didn't know . . .
TESSA.   What do you want to know things like that for . . . *(FLANAGAN
    comforts her.)*
LILLY.   Robert . . . Come here . . . What are you thinking? *(ROBERT sits
    beside her.)*
ROBERT.   I was thinking up a new plot . . . I think I've got a good one . . .
    really . . . If we ever get out of this alive . . .
LILLY.   Tell me about it . . .
ROBERT.   No, I always tell you about it . . . And that just unwinds it . . . I must
    keep this one — close . . . When I tell you it doesn't work any more . . . I
    realise that . . . After twelve years I realise that . . . I know how to write my
    books . . . Like I wrote my first one . . . *(Getting excited.)* I never told anyone
    about that . . . Not a word . . . I've been telling you about every bloody
    thought I've had since we met!
LILLY.   Sharing . . .
ROBERT.   I've been sharing the wrong things . . . Before I had your
    encouragement I could write . . . I was alone! I could write . . . But since I've
    had you encouraging me . . . It sapped me . . .
LILLY.   Bob . . .
ROBERT.   Oh don't . . . don't . . . If we die we die alone . . . That's what made
    me realise . . . Essentially we live alone . . . There must be one part of us that
    links . . .
MR DIMITRY.   To God . . . That's how I see it . . . excuse me . . . You've got
    to save something wild . . . If you domesticate us completely we become
    more dangerous . . . There must always be a part of us that is wild . . . It's
    disappearing . . . It took me forty years to learn to swear in front of my wife
    . . . isn't that right darling?
MRS DIMITRY.   That's right . . .
MR DIMITRY.   Shit!
MRS DIMITRY.   He's only upsetting himself not me . . . I don't care . . . I
    don't give a shit . . . You're not going to trap me with these taboo words . . . I
    just don't need to use them — there's no other reason . . .
MR DIMITRY.   Haven't I been more wild since I converted to our Lord?
MRS DIMITRY.   You've certainly been more irrational . . .
MR DIMITRY.   I answer to a deeper call — that's why . . . I even go for long

walks without taking the dog . . . why should I take him all the time . . . ?

MRS DIMITRY. I have to hire a man to take the dog for a walk.

MR DIMITRY. We can afford it . . . Don't you realise I'm fighting for a principle?

MRS DIMITRY. Oh yes . . . He never bit you . . . It's OK by me honeybun . . .

MR DIMITRY. And its OK by me honeybun . . .

MRS DIMITRY. You always been good to me . . .

MRS DIMITRY (*to the others*). She's got a wild character . . . That's what first attracted me to the Lord . . . I could see it in her . . . Be a mortician she told me when I was a council clerk . . . I said the town is crammed with morticians . . . She says they're dying off like flies now's the time to move in . . . Now where did she get that urge . . . (*FLANAGAN and his wife have moved off to be more alone.*)

FLANAGAN. You might have told me . . .

TESSA. You married a dumb dumb . . . and a selfish girl . . . you want to marry a slut as well?

FLANAGAN. I always told you the truth about me . . .

TESSA. It didn't help . . . What good's the truth when it's wrecking lives?

FLANAGAN. I married you . . . I knew what you were . . . I met you in a night-club . . . You were a stripper remember . . . Since you married me you've pretended you're something else . . .

TESSA. I want to be something else . . . I want to be something else . . .

ROBERT (*to* LILLY). Do you really want to know the idea? The plot?

LILLY. No . . . For God's sake . . .

ROBERT. Aren't you interested?

LILLY. Of course I'm interested . . . But I don't want to spoil it for you . . .

ROBERT. Well I was going to test the idea on you . . .

LILLY. What does it matter what I think? I'm only a foolish woman . . . a gossip columnist . . . who can while away a wasted hour . . . for some hen-pecking biddies who read my tripe . . . I can give them the never ending prick tease of the flirty married journalist . . . risking all to bring home the bacon . . . Not quite jumping into bed with every horny film star . . . but letting everybody know what a free, liberated woman I am . . . I'm an old cow . . . a frustrated old cow . . . what do you want my ideas for? I can't do anything for you and you certainly can't do anything for me . . .

ROBERT. We've got too used to each other . . .

LILLY. I don't care . . .

ROBERT. The basic idea is that we know who the killer is at the beginning . . . in the archaeology story you know . . .

LILLY. No!

ROBERT. Oh . . . (ROBERT *hurt, moves away from her.*)

MICHAEL (*to no one in particular*). We're going to die . . .

Sound of helicopter approaching. Swooping low. As several run to doorway.

FLANAGAN. It's a chopper! It's a security machine! Jesus look at 'em up there! Like James Bond and Company . . . (*He exits shouting and waving*) Hey! Hey! Hey! (*Sound of rifle shot. Just outside.* FLANAGAN *returns unhurt.*) They don't want us out there . . . There's a whole tribe of them . . .

They're just sitting around in jeeps and rovers. *(Sound of several shots.*
FLANAGAN *looks out, keeping shelter of doorway.)* They're taking
popshots at the 'copter . . . *(Sound of helicopter recedes.)* Oh well . . . they
know we're in trouble here . . .

BILL.   They'll radio for help now . . . Should be about two hours . . .

UMBOKO *and* SUBABA *run in.* SUBABA *tries to set fire to the room, but*
UMBOKO *restrains him. They argue in African dialect.* UMBOKO *persuades*
him not to. SUBABA *exits.*

UMBOKO.   He wanted to set fire to the room . . .

BILL.   With us inside it? That's not the arrangement is it?

UMBOKO.   No . . . Don't worry . . . Some of them are drinking whisky . . .

BILL.   If you've got any sense Umboko you'll scat while you've got the chance
    . . . *(*UMBOKO *removes his head dress.)*

UMBOKO.   That sure is hot man . . . I didn't make that . . . I'd have put
    ventilation in it . . . How long do you give the security forces?

BILL.   Two hours . . . I wouldn't lie to you . . .

UMBOKO.   So this is then end of our association . . . By the way . . . *(He gives*
    BILL *money in notes.)* This was on Pike . . . I know it's come from you . . .

BILL.   Thank you . . .

UMBOKO *(bringing out a small book).*   You better sign for it . . .

BILL.   Of course . . . *(He signs.)*

UMBOKO.   We don't go in for looting . . .

BILL.   If you ever want a job . . . after all this . . .

UMBOKO.   If you ever want a job . . .

BILL.   I'll give you a good reference . . .

UMBOKO.   We'll need a good tourist industry man . . . I'll be looking for a
    white hunter . . .

BILL.   Really?

UMBOKO.   That's going to be my job . . . Minister for tourism . . . I got it
    already . . . That's why I don't want too much bloodshed man . . . I got to put
    this thing together afterwards . . .

BILL.   Of course . . . You'll win . . . *(Shots off, couple of whoops.)*

UMBOKO.   Don't worry about them cowboys . . . They don't know how to
    behave . . .

BILL.   I was surprised at Subaba . . .

UMBOKO.   He's got a Prime Minister complex he has . . . Well I gotta be
    going . . . we gotta hightail it out of here pretty quick . . .

BILL.   Are you to the Left or Right of those being hung?

UMBOKO.   Left . . .

BILL.   Will there be any room for private enterprise later?

UMBOKO.   Plenty . . . within the state control . . .

BILL.   I ask for one thing when you gain power . . . I just want the name 'Big
    Bill Safari Enterprises' to survive . . . I don't care who owns the — the equity
    . . .

UMBOKO.   I'll fix it *(*BILL *and* UMBOKO *shake hands.)* Lie low . . . Don't
    come out for an hour . . . Don't provoke anything . . . Wait till we're well
    clear . . .

BILL.   What about my trucks?

UMBOKO.   We need 'em . . . You get government compensation — You get new ones.

BILL (*surprised to hear this*).   Oh . . .

UMBOKO.   Or money in kind . . . I been into that . . . there's a leaflet in the kitchen drawer . . . *(Puts on his mask again. Hesitates. Does wild leap into centre of room.)*

MRS DIMITRY.   Quick Wilmer! You must get that!

MR DIMITRY.   Got it! *(*WILMER *takes flash of* UMBOKO. UMBOKO *exits.)*

BILL *(about* UMBOKO*).*   He's a nice chap really . . . Got in with these Nationalist chaps . . . like the Scots . . . Well now I suggest . . . what do I suggest . . . I suggest that we do nothing . . . have another drink . . . Have a sandwich . . . and wait for help to arrive . . . *(*FLANAGAN *goes over to the door.)*

FLANAGAN.   They're still out there . . . drinking . . .

BILL.   I don't like that . . . They'll have to skedaddle soon . . .

FLANAGAN.   They don't seem to know what to do . . . With their new found freedom . . . Tiger masks and jeeps . . . machine guns . . . helmets . . . What a mixture . . . *(He walks away from the door.)*

MICHAEL.   We should run for it . . . We must break out . . . If we all go out different ways . . . Some will get away . . .

BILL.   Nonsense . . .

MICHAEL.   They've soaked the place with petrol . . .

BILL.   That was a precaution . . .

MICHAEL.   It would only take a spark . . .

BILL.   Alright I shan't — shan't smoke over there . . . Yes — good point . . . *(Goes to door — looks out.)* They'll be away any moment . . . Of course we still mustn't go out you know . . . because there's animals around . . . Not without firearms . . .

FLANAGAN.   It pays to advertise . . .

BILL.   Don't underestimate the wild life out here . . . It moves . . . sometimes it's here . . . suddenly it's gone . . . nomads . . . nomadic . . . *(Sound of jeeps etc, revving up.)*

ROBERT.   They're going . . .

FLANAGAN.   They're not . . .

Sounds cut — as they switch off engines again.

BILL.   False alarm . . . They're getting restless . . . they'll be away . . . Come away from the door . . . they'll forget all about us . . . they'll be off soon

ROBERT.   One of them's going round the back . . . *(They wait. Sound off, kitchen direction. Breaking china. Pause.* ROBERT *still at door.)* Here he comes . . .

BILL.   More whisky?

ROBERT.   Yes . . .

BILL.   Wish I hadn't kept such a stock of it in . . . Still I expect old Umboko's signing for it all . . . it's the other one I don't like — Subaba . . . the one with the Prime Minster complex . . . he takes it all much too seriously . . .

FLANAGAN (*to* FRED).   How does this trouble affect your business?

FRED.   Oh there's plenty of money to be made out of a blockade . . . more middle-men . . . It has to come through more people . . . everything . . . That's why I needed a break . . . Get away from it all . . . it's all so complicated . . . Don't you find that today? Modern life?

FLANAGAN.   It's so complicated that rats like you can make a pile . . .

FRED.   True . . . I didn't ask to be insulted . . .

FLANAGAN.   Well you're living off the rest of us aren't you? What do you contribute?

FRED.   I try and love my fellow man . . .

FLANAGAN.   Which one . . .

FRED.   I could back a picture of yours you know . . . I could easily help you finance a film . . .

FLANAGAN.   I don't need you . . .

FRED.   Many people have said that and lived to regret it . . .

MICHAEL.   I've said it . . .

FRED.   And you need me don't you . . .

MICHAEL.   Yes . . . I need your employment . . . till the end of the month . . .

FRED.   Oh am I being given notice? Oh this is thrilling . . .

MICHAEL.   You hired me as a private secretary remember . . .

FRED.   My dear boy you are a most private secretary . . .

MICHAEL.   That's my job . . . I don't get paid for my friendship . . . that's given . . .

FRED.   Did I ever suggest anything else?

MICHAEL.   You know I can't type . . . You know I can't keep enagements . . . I don't know where your things are . . . Shouldn't I know things like that if I'm a private secretary . . . Shouldn't I know what you're doing tomorrow and the day after? Well shouldn't I?

FRED.   You've got to be able to learn on the job . . .

MICHAEL.   Learn? Learn what? Learn that I'm no good to anybody and that I never have been . . . Well am I your private secretary or not?

FRED.   Don't be silly . . .

MICHAEL.   Well dictate a letter to me . . . One little letter . . .

FRED (*to the others*).   You see . . . you see . . . I have him standing by . . . correspondence? He's ready for it . . .

MICHAEL.   Stop laughing at me! They all know what I am . . . *(MICHAEL runs out. Sleeping accommodation side.)*

BILL (*calls after him*).   It's better we all stay in here . . .

FRED.   I think he wants a rise . . .

FLANAGAN.   We know what he wants . . .

FRED.   Well don't get on at me . . . I'm not a profiteer. I'm as human as you are . . . I can't help making money . . . It doesn't matter what I buy up out of kindness . . . it seems to turn into some sort of goldmine . . . I try and give a boy a start in life . . . I try . . .

There is a shot off, where MICHAEL *has gone.* BILL *exits. pause. Comes back with small revolver.*

BILL.   I didn't know there were more arms about . . . We might have used this

earlier . . . to good effect . . . *(MR DIMITRY moves to door.)* No don't go in
. . . He's had it . . .

MRS DIMITRY.   What is it?

MR DIMITRY.   The boy Michael . . . he shot himself . . .

MRS DIMITRY.   Oh dear . . . I wanted to talk to him . . .

MR DIMITRY.   I told him about our son, Doris . . .

MRS DIMITRY.   That would have helped . . .

MR DIMITRY.   It didn't help enough . . . I told him I was to blame . . . I should
have told him I was to blame for his sins as well — because I am . . .

FLANAGAN.   What are you trying to become — Jesus Christ?

MR DIMITRY.   Yes . . . I'm a long way from goal . . . *(To* MRS DIMITRY.*)*
Mother we've got to get back home . . . we've got to get these pictures back
home . . . we gotta get up that penitentiary and cheer up that lad . . . I think
we're away too long . . . mother . . . *(She comforts him.)* I tried to reach
him . . .

FLANAGAN.   What do we need blacks for? When we can do it to each
other?

*Sound of jeeps revving up. This time they drive off. BILL goes off — verandah
side. Comes back in.*

BILL.   They've gone . . .

Curtain.